DISCARDED
From Nashville Public Library

SCRUM MASTERY

Geoff Watts

SCRUM MASTERY

From Good To Great Servant Leadership

Copyright, Inspect & Adapt Ltd 2013-2021

All Rights Reserved. No part of this publication may be reproduced, stored in or introduced into a retrieval system, or transmitted, in any form, or by any means (electronic, mechanical, photocopying, recording or otherwise) without the prior written permission of the publisher. Any person who does any unauthorised act in relation to this publication may be liable for criminal prosecution and civil claims for damages.

This book is sold subject to the condition that it shall not, by way of trade or otherwise, be lent, re-sold, hired out, or otherwise circulated without the publisher's prior consent in any form or binding or cover other than that in which it is published and without a similar condition including this condition being imposed on the subsequent purchaser.

Second Edition Published March 2021
First Edition Published 2013 by Inspect & Adapt Ltd
96 Redgrove Park, Cheltenham, Glos, GL51 6QZ

Edited by Rebecca Traeger

Design by Ole H. Størksen

All illustrations from Shutterstock.com
Main illustrations by and based on the works of Dan Cristo/Shutterstock.
Cover illustration Vectomart and Dan Cristo/Shutterstock.

ISBN: 9798733307589

Dedicated to

My wife Alison, my daughter Freya and my sons Cody and Grayson

Hopefully this book will explain a little better than
I have previously managed to do myself what my job has been
for the last twenty years or so.

You are my inspiration

I love you guys

Table of Contents

Foreword by Mike Cohn	9
Foreword by Esther Derby	12
Acknowledgements	14
Introduction - Why This Book?	17
Why The Second Edition	21
Get RE-TRAINED for Success	25
RESPECTED	31
Above All, Empower The Team	37
Keeping The Peace?	43
Holding To Account	51
ENABLING	59
The Bulls**t Buzzer	65
The Problem With Proxies	71
Be Selfish to be Generous	79
TACTFUL	89
A Tale Of Two Scrums	93
How Long Is a Piece Of String?	99
The Power of Silence	105
RESOURCEFUL	111
Sex Up Your Scrum	115
Be ADAPTIVE in Retrospectives	123
The Repetitive Retrospective	133

ALTERNATIVE	141
T-Shaped People	145
Getting Stuff "Done"	157
Review The Sprint Review	165
INSPIRING	173
Invoking Creativity	177
Sprint Goals	185
Burn The Burndown?	195
NURTURING	201
The Problem Team	205
Growing Individuals or SQUADs?	213
Assess Your Way To Maturity	219
Remote Control Scrum	229
EMPATHIC	241
Two Ears, One Mouth	245
Yes, But That Will Never Work	251
Coaching For Change	257
DISRUPTIVE	269
Forgiveness & Permission	273
Eliminating Distractions	281
Surviving The Corporate Culture	289
An ORGANIC Culture	295
HAVE BELIEF	304
Index	321
References	328

Foreword by Mike Cohn

I first met Geoff Watts at the 2004 Scrum Gathering in Boulder. Back then Scrum Gatherings were invitation-only events for the foremost practitioners of what was starting to become the leading agile approach. Shortly after that Scrum Gathering, Geoff became the first Certified Scrum Trainer in the UK, and today he is one of the most respected in the world.

I was honored when Geoff asked me to write a foreword for this book as it covers a topic very important to me: Lots of Scrum teams and ScrumMasters are good, but very few become great. Since its publication, Scrum Mastery: From Good To Great Servant Leadership has changed that and this updated edition will further that change.

Geoff brings to this book a wealth of experience—he was a ScrumMaster and agile coach with BT (British Telecom) during their transition to agile, one of the world's first large-scale Scrum adoptions. Since then, as a consultant, he has worked with large and small organisations in various stages of transitioning to Scrum. Geoff's wealth of experience shows through in the advice he offers us here.

In this book, Geoff speaks to good ScrumMasters who wish to be great. He summarizes key points by saying "A good ScrumMaster does this; a great ScrumMaster does that." I loved this. Not only does it keep his writing direct and on point, I found it reminiscent of the Agile Manifesto and its statements of valuing "this over that."

> *A good book reinforces what we know;*
> *a great book teaches us something new.*

I've been involved with Scrum projects since 1995. And, although there's always more to learn, most books rehash well-trod territory and I don't finish them any wiser. Scrum Mastery: From Good To Great Servant Leadership gave me several new ideas. For example, in writing about the sprint review, Geoff offers a set of questions that can be asked at every sprint review. These questions — Have priorities changed? Have any estimates changed? — are all ones I've asked before. But I don't think I've ever asked all of them in the same review, and I've never thought of having a key set of questions to go over in each review. I've since enjoyed trying this with some of the teams I work.

A good book is worth reading; a great book is worth coming back to.

In the eight years since it was released, I have referred back to this book many times and will continue to do so in the years to come. Like Scrum itself, many of the core ideas here are simple—ensure teams have access to their product owners, let teams make decisions, know the power of silence. But there are nuances to these simplicities and I've returned to the book to re-read Geoff's explanations and tips.

A good book is easy to read; a great book makes you forget you're reading at all and comes alive in our heads.

We visualize what's happening. That's a particularly challenging goal in a technical book. Through the numerous stories throughout Scrum Mastery, Geoff pulls us in, introducing us to the ScrumMasters and team members he has encountered in his career. Just as Geoff learned from them, we learn from Geoff telling their stories.

A good book makes you think; a great book gives you new things to think about.

You will, of course, find the usual Scrum topics here—retrospectives, collaboration, sprint reviews, and the like. Along the way you'll also be challenged with new ways to think about these topics, such as how a weather forecast may be better than a burndown chart and why a story pint may be better than a story point. And Geoff's British sense of humor makes learning about it all the more entertaining.

A good author is worth reading;
a great author is worth reading even when you disagree with him.

Do I agree with everything in here? Of course not. Too much of being a great ScrumMaster depends on one's personal style. But even when I disagreed with a suggestion, Geoff's writing and arguments were strong enough to make me stop and reconsider my own views.

As ScrumMasters, we should all value being great over being good. Scrum Mastery: From Good To Great Servant Leadership offers us plenty of advice for achieving it.

Mike Cohn
Author of Succeeding with Agile
Boulder, Colorado

Foreword by Esther Derby

As Geoff points out in the introduction to Scrum Mastery: From Good To Great Servant-Leadership, there is no unequivocal definition of the role of ScrumMaster. In fact, there's little more than the directive, "do everything possible to help the team be productive." How to do this is left up to each individual.

This ambiguity is both a blessing and a curse. It is a blessing when it allows for creative solutions and local adaptations that are appropriate to the circumstances. It's a curse when the lack of specificity allows old mental models and patterns of behaviour to persist under a new name. If you imagine the only way to increase productivity is carrots and sticks, those are the tools you'll use, no matter what your title is.

Every team is alike in some ways and different in others. Agile teams are alike in that they strive to work cross-functionally to deliver working software. Many of them work in iterations. But from there, differences abound. Some teams need to learn solid engineering practices. Others need help with a specific skill such as automated unit testing. Still others need coaching to become a functioning team. Many need help making the mental shift to working in feature-slices that fit into short iterations. A ScrumMaster may need completely different skills depending on the team and the organization.

But what a ScrumMaster always needs are the qualities that Geoff describes in this book:

Resourceful in removing impediments to productivity
Enabling, helping others be effective
Tactful, diplomacy personified

Respected, known for integrity both within the team and in the wider organization
Alternative, prepared to promote a counter-culture
Inspiring, generating enthusiasm and energy in others
Nurturing of both individuals and teams
Empathic, sensitive to those around them
Disruptive, able to shift the old status quo and help create a new way of working

These are the qualities that guide a ScrumMaster towards servant-leadership rather than command and control.

I have had the privilege of watching Geoff in action. He truly has a gift for connecting, and coaching without judgement or impatience. His insights and fine touch with people and teams shine through in the stories you will read in Scrum Mastery.

Of course, dear reader, you will, and should, find your own path and make use of your own unique talents and gifts. With Geoff's experiences and stories as a guide, you will see that a ScrumMaster is not master of the team, but a master at encouraging, enabling, and energizing people to gel as a team and realize their full potential.

Esther Derby
Co-author of Agile Retrospectives
Duluth, Minnesota

Acknowledgements

There are many great people who have contributed to this book; some of them consciously and some quite inadvertently.

The first people I would like to mention are all from my time at BT where I started using Scrum in anger. The first person I would like to mention is my old boss Denis Lee (with one n !!) who always believed in me and tolerated my counter-culture ideas, trusting my instincts. I also don't think I would have gotten very far with Scrum if it weren't for my first product owner, Mike Lynch. And then there was Sean O'Donovan who even supported me when I knew it was time to leave and go it alone. Without you guys, I wouldn't have begun collecting these experiences and stories. Thank you.

I'm very grateful for those who have heard and read my stories over the years. Some, in particular have even helped me by analysing and reviewing them formally for this book including Mike Cohn, Esther Derby, Roman Pichler and Jean Tabaka. I'm not sure they realised what they were letting themselves in for when agreeing to help but you all stuck with me. Your compassionately brutal feedback has helped me to find, redefine and refine my way! Thank you

Paul Goddard should be in the list above but I want to reserve special thanks for him. He's always been there to listen to my latest crazy ideas or create a new game with me and much of what is written here has gone through the Goddard filter at some point or another. Thank you.

Possibly the most obvious people to thank are all the ScrumMasters and teams that I've worked with who have effectively given me the material. Some of you may be able to pick out your story and I thank you all for your openness and the opportunities you gave me to work with you. Thank you.

I should also mention my twitter followers who joined in the "good & great" discussions and also helped with my efforts to choose the book design. This brings me on to Ole Størksen, a fantastic designer from Norway who had to tolerate working with my severely limited imagination to produce something that looks even better than I could have ever imagined. Thank you.

The one person that I knew, without question, had to be a part of this project was Rebecca Traeger. She is a tremendous editor who put in a lot of work to turn my ramblings and musings into something that could actually be understood! And not just the once either! As the book took various forms, she helped re-organise and maintain consistency. I am so grateful that she agreed to be part of this project. Thank you.

And then, of course, there is my family; my wife, my children and my in-laws who have had to put up with the many nights of me being away from home, the confusion about what I actually do for a living ("what job do you do Daddy that involves spaghetti, plastic balls and Lego?"), and the times when I have taken myself away to concentrate on my writing. They have always supported me and the decisions that I have made. Knowing that I have such a great supporting unit behind me and believing in me has made this so much easier. Thank you.

Introduction - Why This Book?

*"There go the people.
I must follow them for I am their leader."*
Alexandre Ledru-Rollin

For too many organisations, Scrum has been a big disappointment; a failed experiment that hasn't delivered anywhere near the positive impact that management were hoping for. Yet I have also witnessed the great rewards and transformative power that come when a company truly embraces Scrum concepts and agile principles. What's the difference between success and failure for organisations that adopt a servant-leader approach like Scrum? How effective their ScrumMasters are in the role.

I fundamentally believe in both the power and also the humanising nature of self-managing, empowered teams and I am equally sure that the key to achieving these benefits is the ScrumMaster. Put simply, if organisations can create and support great ScrumMasters then those ScrumMasters will foster great teams and create environments that enable these teams to create great products. This book aims to give ScrumMasters the tools to go from good to great, bringing your team and organisation to higher levels in the process.

I feel great sympathy for many of the people who find themselves in the ScrumMaster role as it is very difficult, often misunderstood and there is very little specific guidance on how to perform the role well. They are also often swimming against the tide of traditional management techniques from the 20th Century, which are not fit for today's age of rapid change and complexity.

I look back to my early days as a newly minted ScrumMaster, absolutely loving the opportunity to help my team grow and my organisation become more effective, even though there was precious little specific advice on how to do my job well. Twenty years later, after working with many agile teams as ScrumMaster, internal coach, external coach and consultant, I have been lucky to observe and work with many great ScrumMasters and Scrum teams and have learned a lot from them. I have identified key practices and patterns that great ScrumMasters exhibit. I present them throughout this book as phrases that describe the fine line between good ScrumMasters and great ones.

Notice that the difference is between good and great—not bad and good—both sets of characteristics in the stories that follow are positive. This is similar to the way that the agile manifesto sets out its values, e.g. "Individuals and Interactions over Processes and Tools" [1]. At no point is the agile manifesto attempting to suggest that processes and tools are bad; all it is trying to suggest is that individuals and interactions are considered more valuable.

The stories that fill this book are drawn from real experiences of real ScrumMasters in real teams—only the names and details have been changed.

At its core, Scrum aims to harness the power of self-managing, autonomous, engaged teams who take responsibility for delivery and collaborate directly with their customers. These fantastic delivery teams do not just magically appear but are created, nurtured and supported by servant-leader ScrumMasters. Read on to find out how to raise the bar of Scrum in your organisation and your own personal bar of Scrum Mastery as well.

Why The Second Edition?

There have been a few changes to the Scrum Guide over the last eight years and so I have updated small references to parts of the framework that have changed but the bigger reason for a new version is the addition of new content.

I have added four new stories that reflect other important aspects of the ScrumMaster role that have become more important over the last few years. In particular, how to adopt a more professional coaching stance at the individual level (See *Coaching for Change*) as well as effect change in the organisational culture and structure (See *An ORGANIC Culture*).

Additionally, I have seen ScrumMasters overplay their people-pleasing traits, leading to a dependency upon them from the team and burnout in the individual. Hence the story *Be Selfish to be Generous*. And finally distributed teams were always a reality for many organisations but since the Coronavirus pandemic of 2020, remote working became the norm for almost everyone and so I shared a story of Scrum Mastery with a remote team (See *Remote Control Scrum*).

I have also re-organised the chapters a little from the original edition. This is mostly to share out the chapters more equally among the RETRAINED sections and I took advantage of the fact that many stories showed multiple Scrum Mastery characteristics and so were equally at home in more than one section.

I have been blown away by the messages of appreciation and gratitude I have received from thousands of readers of Scrum Mastery and the fact that this is now a staple book in training courses around the world and even university courses is something of which I am immensely proud. Overall, I believe this is an even more comprehensive guide to being a ScrumMaster and I hope you find it just as valuable as the first edition.

Introduction – Why The Second Edition?

Servant-leaders serve first and then come to lead. Their best test is "do those served grow as persons?"

Get RE-TRAINED for Success

A good ScrumMaster grasps the responsibilities of the role.
A great ScrumMaster grasps the skills and mindset of the role.

I don't think I have ever come across a job role that has been so popular yet simultaneously derided; so simple yet so misunderstood; so common-sense and yet so revolutionary as the ScrumMaster.

The role's introduction was intended to be somewhat controversial. The ScrumMaster role offers neither authority nor an attractive title. As a result, those who want a powerful position, as opposed to a leadership role, tend not to apply.

A ScrumMaster is part facilitator, part coach and part coordinator. They are also part parent, part orchestra conductor and part sheepdog. And much, much more. The ScrumMaster should do whatever is needed to help the team become high performing and for the organisation to deliver excellent products quickly. For this reason, it is incredibly hard to nail down a definition of the role. What a ScrumMaster needs to do one sprint could be incredibly different from what they need to do in the next sprint. From the earliest days of Scrum, the ScrumMaster has always been described as a servant-leader for the team. A ScrumMaster should serve the product owner, the developers and the organisation in various ways, most notably in facilitation, impediment removal and coaching. This definition of a servant-leader helps add some certainty and solidity to the ambiguous statement of "do whatever is needed."

What Is a Servant-Leader?

The term servant-leadership originated from an essay by Robert K. Greenleaf in 1970, "The Servant As Leader" [2] where he essentially calls for a reversal of traditional leadership (the accumulation and exercise of power by one person at the top of the pyramid). Instead, Greenleaf calls for a leader whose focus is to ensure that other people's highest priority needs are being served. The guiding principle of servant leadership states that "the highest priority of a servant-leader is to encourage, support and enable subordinates to unfold their full potential and abilities."

Servant-leaders serve first and then come to lead. Their best test, as Greenleaf describes it, is "do those served grow as persons? Do they, while being served, become healthier, wiser, freer, more autonomous, more likely themselves to become servants?" I encourage everyone to read Greenleaf's essay and be amazed at how relevant his words are to a world fifty plus years after he wrote them.

Greenleaf identified the toxic culture created by an hierarchical structure where one person sits atop the pyramid. Such a system, Greenleaf argued, "gives control priority over leadership" and "nourishes the notion among able people that one must be the boss to be effective" encouraging "a pernicious and petty status striving that corrupts everyone."

Greenleaf knew this change would be hard – indeed we still haven't seen the societal change he hoped for – and so the task for the ScrumMaster within a traditional organisation is also hard. But just because something is hard, does not mean it is to be avoided. Indeed, as John F. Kennedy said in 1962, "We choose to go to the Moon [...] and do the other things, not because they are easy, but because they are hard, because that goal will serve to organise and measure the best of our energies and skills, because that challenge is one that we are willing to accept, one we are unwilling to postpone, and one which we intend to win."

What Do I Mean By Great?

In his book, *Good to Great: Why Some Companies Make the Leap and Others Don't,* Jim Collins [3] describes Level 5 Leaders:

"Level 5 leaders look out the window to apportion credit to factors outside themselves when things go well. At the same time, they look in the mirror to apportion responsibility, never blaming bad luck when things go poorly."

Like Collins, Greenleaf refers to servant-leaders in a similar manner when he says "The servant views any problem in the world as inside oneself, not out there. And if a flaw in the world is to be remedied, to the servant the process of change starts in the servant."

These leaders are highly ambitious but not for themselves; instead, they want their organisations to excel. They build successors rather than try to set people up to fail to make themselves look good. Great ScrumMasters share the characteristics of Level 5 leaders.

Being a great servant-leader calls for a certain set of characteristics:

RESOURCEFUL
They are creative in removing impediments to productivity

ENABLING
They are passionate about helping others be effective

T*ACTFUL*
They are diplomacy personified

R*ESPECTED*
They have a reputation for integrity both within the team and in the wider organisation

A*LTERNATIVE*
They are prepared to promote a counter-culture

I*NSPIRING*
They generate enthusiasm and energy in others

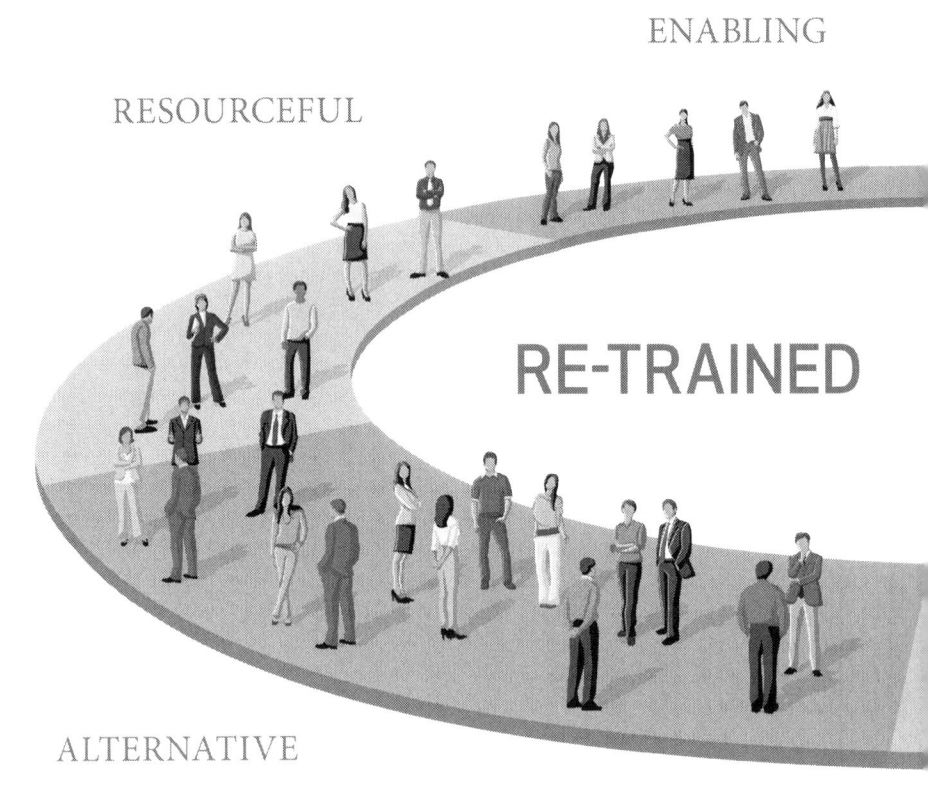

ENABLING

RESOURCEFUL

RE-TRAINED

ALTERNATIVE

INSPIRING

Nurturing
They enjoy helping both individuals and teams develop and grow

Empathic
They are sensitive to those around them

Disruptive
They break the old status quo and help create a new way of working

You can think of these characteristics in the context of the acronym RE-TRAINED. Over the course of this book, we will look at how great ScrumMasters have exemplified and can develop these characteristics.

RETRAINED

Respected

"It is far better to be trusted and respected than to be liked."

Jean Dickinson (my Grandmother)

One of the first things to learn about the ScrumMaster role is that it holds no authority. ScrumMasters are expected to embody Scrum values and principles, facilitate the adoption of the process, guide the growth of the team and act as change agents for the organisation—all with no real formal power. Therefore, in order to be effective as a ScrumMaster it is imperative to earn the respect not only of the team but also of influential people within the organisation. Great ScrumMasters have good relationships with the team and can build rapport with others quickly and strongly. This allows them to facilitate effectively in trying circumstances and ask the tough questions that will encourage critical reflection within the team.

In one workshop I was running for a new project team, I was asked how to find the best ScrumMasters. As is my wont, I flipped the question back on them and, after we had clarified the responsibilities of the role, I asked the group to elect their ScrumMaster. I gave everyone in the room (about 25 people) a number of blank index cards and asked them to write the names of anyone who they thought would make a great ScrumMaster on an index card (one name per card). The cards were placed in a box so that I could count the votes. Of the 25 people, 23 had picked the same person. It seemed that this group knew instinctively who would make a great ScrumMaster. Every time I have run this exercise, I have had similar results.

Teams are surprisingly consistent in choosing who will be good at enabling them to be effective; they know who will get the best out of them. It is also often very different from the person that management tends to select for the role! Given that the team is not accountable to the ScrumMaster and, if anything the ScrumMaster is accountable to the team, it makes a certain amount of sense for the ScrumMaster to be chosen by the team. You might even go so far as to suggest that if the ScrumMaster isn't doing a good job as a servant-leader, then the team should find themselves a new ScrumMaster.

Respected ScrumMasters all seem to have a humility about them; a certain selflessness and lack of ego that increases their integrity and the respect they are given. Humble ScrumMasters take regular time-outs to reflect on who has helped them improve their talents or be successful. They acknowledge the mistakes they have made and identify where others have been successful without their help or, better still, in spite of their contributions. To mindfully practice humility, try asking for help and admitting where you have gaps in your knowledge.

Respected ScrumMasters have a much greater rate of success in removing impediments and enabling change within the wider organisation as their views have greater weight with the influence-holders. Being chosen by the team indicates a level of respect that immediately puts new ScrumMasters on a positive footing in their attempts to serve, coach and mould their teams into high-performing units. Perhaps it won't be long before we see some ScrumMaster election campaigns in the offices of agile organisations!

TIP During the next retrospective, ask for feedback from the team on how you could become a better ScrumMaster. Not only will you get some great ideas for how to improve but also merely the act of asking for feedback tends to increase respect. Share your values with the team and ask them to help you keep from compromising them.

A huge element of respect comes from having integrity. Integrity involves honesty, consistency, reliability and a strong moral code. If you have integrity then people know what they can expect from you and (usually) appreciate both who you are and the certainty that gives them.

Why is this useful to a Scrum team?

Scientific studies have proven that people are hard-wired against uncertainty. A UCLA study reported on by David Rock [1] using functional MRI scans has indicated that, when faced with uncertainty or ambiguity, the same parts of the brain light up that are stimulated by physical pain. Scrum introduces (or makes explicit) a lot of uncertainty—around requirements, process, hierarchy, job descriptions amongst other things—so having someone you can rely on is highly desirable. The ScrumMaster can be the rock in the storm for the team.

When people know where they stand with the ScrumMaster, it fosters trust and respect. Team members are more likely to come to a respected ScrumMaster with their issues, concerns and impediments. This in turn increases the strength of the ScrumMaster's hand when facilitating - remember they have little authority.

TIP Don't over-promise but, instead, make many small commitments and keep them. Admit and apologise, without making excuses, when you fail to keep your commitment.

"You might even suggest that if the ScrumMaster isn't doing a good job, then the team should find themselves a new servant-leader"

Chris could probably have slipped out of the office unnoticed and the team would have been just fine

Above All, Empower the Team

*A good ScrumMaster will be indispensable to a team.
A great ScrumMaster will become both
dispensable and wanted.*

One of the most effective ways for ScrumMasters to gain respect is to deliberately not take control. For someone starting out in the role of ScrumMaster, I offer two basic pieces of advice. You could consider them the two commandments of a ScrumMaster.

1. First Ask The Team

Whatever the question is and no matter how difficult the problem is, your default response should always be, "I'm going to ask the team what they think we should do." This is more easily said than done because most people's (unconscious) response is, "OK, what's the answer? How do I solve this?"

In addition to asking direct questions to solve problems, I also encourage the ScrumMaster to ask the team to reflect on situations, both real and abstract, to discover important learning points. Possibly one of the best people at this, so I have read, was Phil Jackson, the former coach of the Chicago Bulls and Los Angeles Lakers. As well as being an incredibly successful coach, Jackson was known for deliberately encouraging this type of reflection through some fairly abstract coaching techniques. For example, he was not averse to showing the players videos or giving them a book to read and asking them to find a message that would be of use to the team's development or performance.

2. Make Yourself Redundant

My second piece of advice is to go into the role of ScrumMaster with the intention of making the role of ScrumMaster for this team unnecessary. Create such a high-performing, self-managing team, with such a good relationship with the product owner, with such a keen understanding of the Scrum framework (and the principles behind the framework) that they don't need any facilitation (of either process or people) and have no impediments left to remove. In other words, be so great that they don't need you anymore. I'm not saying this will definitely happen, but the more you aim for it, the more quickly your team will develop and the better your team will perform. To go back to Greenleaf's essay, he says:

"The best test, and most difficult to administer, is: Do those served grow as persons? Do they, while being served, become healthier, wiser, freer, more autonomous, more likely themselves to become servants?"

Take the following story about Chris as an example of one such excellent servant-leader.

Chris was the ScrumMaster for Team Hurricane, who were approaching the end of their 20th sprint. As she looked over the burndown charts and retrospective outputs for the previous sprints, she felt a warm glow. She was so proud of how this group of people had really grown into a team, probably the best team she had been part of in her 15-year career.

Looking back, Chris could remember how tough the first couple of sprints were. There was that time when she wondered if Benny and Carl would be able to stay in the same building let alone the same team. And then there was that sprint review when she had been so sure the project would get pulled because the velocity was so low. There was even one point when she thought the team were going to give up completely on Scrum and go back to waterfall. Those early weeks and months had required so much energy, determination and creativity! She had felt at times that she had almost needed to beg the team to attend the meetings, update the burndown chart, and say anything more than the bare minimum in the sprint retrospectives.

Chris smiled at how different things were now. Tomorrow she would be off on maternity leave, but the team had not yet decided whether they would even bother to find someone to fill in for her. They were planning to address it at their retrospective session next Thursday. Even though she would be leaving mid-sprint, Chris felt confident that the team would be fine without her. The fact that they had already lined up what they were going to address in the retrospective was an indication that the team were in control of things. That, coupled with the fact that Saffron, the product owner, was over with the team right now looking through and signing off on the latest features meant that the sprint review was probably going to be as smooth as normal as well.

In fact, if it wasn't for the huge party the team were throwing for her, she could probably have slipped out of the office unnoticed and the team would have been just fine. Chris had accomplished what she'd never thought possible—she'd done such a good job in her role that she was no longer really needed, at least not full-time. What a spectacular problem to have!

Shu-Ha-Ri - or The Hairy Shoe

Shu Ha Ri (or as many people affectionately call it The Hairy Shoe) is best described by reference to the original *The Karate Kid* movie, which I was (rather belatedly) introduced to by my great friend Paul Goddard. In the film, Mr. Miyagi teaches his student, Daniel, karate in a very unconventional way. Rather than teach Daniel karate moves, Mr. Miyagi instead begins by asking him to clean cars, repeating the motion of wax on, wax off. When Daniel, who is in the Shu state of learning, questions the rationale behind this process, Mr. Miyagi tells him, "I say, you do… no questions."

The point of this repetition is to create a new muscle memory so that, without thinking, it can be applied when needed, such as [spoiler alert] when Daniel is attacked. At this moment, Daniel has an epiphany and responds automatically with the wax on, wax off motion he has learned, enabling him to defend himself. As a result of this, he realises the rationale behind all of the repetition. He has now entered the Ha state of learning (which literally means digress or to break from tradition), where he will begin to question the mechanics and find new ways to embody the principles. In the Ha state, the teacher will begin to encourage their student to safely break the rules. Ideally, the student eventually transcends, leaves or separates from the teacher and has no need for the rules (or the teacher). This is the Ri state, where one is effectively no longer the student.

This metaphor is very applicable to Scrum teams and the role of the Scrum-Master. Great ScrumMasters painstakingly guide their teams through these stages of development with the hope of one day creating a team that has no need for a ScrumMaster.

To further expand on this concept, let's look at another film, *Nanny McPhee* [1] about Mr. Brown (a man who has just lost his wife) and his seven badly behaved children. Mr. Brown and his children suffer many unsuccessful nannies before eventually stumbling upon Nanny McPhee, a magical nanny who [spoiler alert #2] manages to teach the children a number of lessons that encourage them to completely alter their behaviour. When Nanny McPhee arrives, she tells the children

"There is something you should understand about the way I work. When you need me but do not want me, then I must stay. When you want me but no longer need me, then I have to go. It's rather sad, really, but there it is."

She then proceeds to change the children's rules and process, restricting their freedom and challenging their authority (for previously they ruled the roost), so much in fact that the children hate the new nanny:

"We will never want you," the children tell her

"Then I shall never leave," replies Nanny McPhee

Eventually, however, the children learn to appreciate the new behaviours that the nanny's rules and process have helped them adopt and enjoy their new lives so much that they don't want her to leave. But she has done her job and so she must leave. Ah, the irony.

Like Nanny McPhee, as you develop as a ScrumMaster and help your team develop through the Shu-Ha-Ri phases and achieve greatness, you too should be ready to leave. "But why would I want to make myself redundant?" you might ask. Why wouldn't you? Imagine putting this on your resume:

> *I enabled a team and an organisation to become so agile and high-performing that I was no longer needed.*

I would argue that if you managed to make yourself redundant you would be in such high demand that this would be the least of your worries!

*Where was Avis?
What was he working on?
Is he actually acting as if he
were a part of this team?*

Keeping The Peace?

*A good ScrumMaster will help maintain team harmony.
A great ScrumMaster will guide a team through disharmony
to reach a new level of teamwork.*

In Patrick Lencioni's leadership fable *The Five Dysfunctions Of A Team* [2] Kathryn, the new CEO of DecisionTech, gathers her team and explains the simple reasons that teams typically fail, the first of which is around trust:

"Great teams do not hold back from one another. [...] They are unafraid to air their dirty laundry. They admit their mistakes, their weaknesses, and their concerns without fear of reprisal."

A major pattern that I have seen with great ScrumMasters is that they help their teams develop a sense of safety where they can be passionately honest and open with one another while remaining within the bounds of respect.

The Jedis are a good example of a team in need of safety. The Jedis were a team about halfway through their first sprint and having their first experiences with Scrum. This was their first project together as a team and, as such, they were just getting used to each other and establishing a working rhythm. The ScrumMaster, Darryl, was also new to Scrum but was chosen to be the ScrumMaster because of his people skills. His history showed he had the ability to bring people together to work effectively as a team.

Sprint planning went relatively well. Everyone was relatively comfortable that what the team had committed to was achievable, and the team seemed motivated by the project. During the sprint Darryl noted that people were focussing on the tasks that they signed up for and were making good progress on them but were still acting fairly independently of one another; there wasn't a great deal of collaboration or teamwork but at least progress was being made. Unfortunately it seemed that Avis, the business analyst on the team, was struggling with a few things. He was often late to the daily scrums and was hard to find during the day when team members had questions about the business process to be implemented.

The team didn't use this as an excuse though and, as was suggested in the training, had self-organised to cope without Avis. They had bypassed him on a number of occasions and had contacted some of his colleagues or the product owner or, in some cases, just worked things out for themselves. The daily scrum, however, was a different matter. As the days passed, Darryl could sense strong frustration growing. Not quite every day, but very often, Avis would turn up five-to-ten minutes late, forcing the team to stop and recap what had been said for Avis' benefit.

What was interesting, from Darryl's point of view, was that the team were not raising this frustration publicly but were keeping their annoyance inside. He could sense a growing resentment toward Avis but didn't think that Avis was aware of it. Darryl knew this was a team issue and one that needed to be solved by the team and so, at the end of the sprint, raised it at the retrospective.

"How did you think the daily scrums worked for you this sprint?" He asked.

Avis was the first to speak out:

"I thought they were really useful. They were a great way for me to catch up with what was going on with the rest of the team. If it wasn't for those meetings I would not have had a clue what everyone else was doing."

"That's good. What about everyone else? Were they useful for everyone?" Darryl asked.

The rest of the team were silent. Perhaps this was still too early for the team to feel safe with each other, or perhaps Avis' comments made it harder for the rest of the team to contradict him but nobody said anything. Darryl then displayed a really useful skill of a ScrumMaster—uncomfortable silence. He waited, and he waited, and when he thought he should say something to move the topic forward, he waited a little longer. Eventually Amie spoke up:

"Well I did think that perhaps we weren't holding them at the right time as they seemed to be a bit awkward for Avis. He was often somewhere else at the start time."

"Thanks Amie. I think it would be useful for us to have a discussion about the start time of the daily scrum in particular and how flexible you want to be on meeting start times in general," Darryl responded.

The team eagerly jumped on that conversation, as it seemed to be a way to change Avis' behaviour without directly confronting him. Unfortunately, Avis' late behaviour continued during the next sprint. At the next retrospective, the problem of latecomers to the daily scrums was brought up yet again. This time, the team decided they would put a fine system in place so anyone who was late for the daily scrum would pay a nominal (£1) fine. Again, Avis continued to turn up late; one day he even turned up with a £20 note to pay his fines in advance! The team had made its point that they expected prompt attendance, but missed the mark on encouraging collaboration. What happened?

Surface The Issue

At the first sprint retrospective, Darryl asked the team about the daily scrum and tried to get the team to bring to the surface how Avis' erratic attendance was affecting them. If Darryl had allowed the problem to fester, the team would have increased their working around of Avis, the assumptions the team were making would probably have got worse and ultimately the resentment of the team towards Avis would have grown, to a potentially damaging level.

Darryl handled the first retrospective well, managing to draw the issues out of the team rather than pushing his ideas on to the team. Allowing the team to voice the issue is far more powerful; letting the silence become uncomfortable is a great tactic for bringing people into the conversation. Darryl also recognised the discomfort of the team members and publicly displayed gratitude for their contribution (thanking Amie and Avis), which is very helpful in encouraging further input from those team members and others.

Darryl didn't have to wait until the retrospective to raise this with the team, though. Scrum actively encourages a team to make daily inspections and adaptations to their working process where necessary. Sometimes teams will fall into the trap of waiting until the end of the sprint to make changes just because they know there is a formal opportunity. Setting the expectation that changes will only occur at the retrospective, although not consciously in this example, can have far-reaching consequences.

In our story, Avis was exhibiting several symptoms of disengagement; coming to the daily scrums late was only one example. Even when this continued into the second sprint, Darryl and the team did not really address the problem until the second retrospective. Additionally, during the first retrospective, Darryl grasped onto the first suggestion that came up, which is typical of a new ScrumMaster. This enabled the team to surface one issue, but it didn't really allow them to explore all of the symptoms or work to solve the root problem. Another major symptom was either ignored or missed—that of Avis being hard to find during the sprint. Where was he? What was he working on? Is he actually acting as if he were a part of this team? Does he have other distractions? I suspect there were deeper issues at play that would have been good to dive into.

Knowing when you've truly reached the core of a problem and when you need to delve deeper comes with experience. Several techniques, such as the "5 Whys," [3] exist to help you and your team move beyond the surface to the real issue. One note of caution, though, these techniques will expose root causes but, in doing so, may cause someone to feel defensive. Use these with care.

Team Formation Stages

In this story, in the terms of the Tuckman model [4], the Jedis were still in the "forming" stage, a time when most team members want to be accepted and avoid confrontation and conflict wherever possible. The forming stage is both a comfortable and frustrating phase of team development. It is comfortable because there is little conflict and because it often occurs in the early stages of the project with little immediate concern over the delivery deadline and thus stress levels are low. It is also frustrating because, due to the lack of conflict, there is actually very little progress or teamwork. Team members are said to be walking on eggshells at this stage, trying harder to not upset each other than to deliver results.

Scrum teams find themselves facing the challenges of working through the team formation stages at a much faster pace and with greater volatility than many traditional teams. This happens because Scrum teams are cross-functional and self-managing and also because of the nature of iterative, incremental delivery. The ScrumMaster should be aware of this and be prepared to help guide a team through these phases of team development quickly. The most successful ScrumMaster interventions that I have seen here have focussed around the facilitation of team norms. For example, clarifying what behaviours the team agree upon and how they wish to handle exceptions. If the team works these agreements out for themselves, they are more likely to stick to them and they will therefore avoid many painful situations (For more on this see the "Holding to Account" chapter).

A harmonious team feels good. There is little stress or tension, nobody's feelings are being hurt, there is little controversy or conflict and people are getting along—at least on the surface. Almost all teams start out like this but, at some point, will move past this into "storming."

When a team is "storming," there is conflict. Conflicting ideas, values, principles and practices will surface as the team attempt to rationalise their identity and each person's place within the team. This is often where the good ScrumMasters separate from the great ScrumMasters. Good ScrumMasters resolve that conflict as easily and quickly as possible, getting a team back to harmony again. This is good because the team cannot function well if they are actively in conflict.

However, great ScrumMasters will use the conflict within the team to move them forward rather than backwards, even though it is almost always a painful process. Working through the conflict to a deep and meaningful resolution takes time and involves careful navigation. It often involves helping the team reflect on the values of each individual within the team and settling on or modifying some team values.

Donuts and Push Ups

I have seen many techniques and tactics from teams as they attempt to deal with the specific example of a latecomer to the daily scrum. Examples include locking the door at the scheduled start time (See Don in "Sex Up Your Scrum") or buying one less donut than there are members of the team. Then there are the forfeits that the latecomer has to pay, things like wearing a cowboy hat, doing push ups or, in the spirit of some of the armed services, making the rest of the team do the push ups while the late attendee watches!

Team formation activities and the establishment of team norms are crucial ScrumMaster's duties. You shouldn't necessarily wait until the retrospective to raise issues to the team if you feel they are affecting the team. You should also avoid taking the first suggestion the team comes up with; instead, keep digging until you are satisfied that the team have covered the real fundamental issue. While it's true that real honesty only comes when the team is mature enough to deal with it, teams need to practice honest reflection in order to mature so it is a delicate balancing act. Beware, however, the team is rarely the best judge of how developed they are as a team and you, as ScrumMaster, will probably find yourself challenging the teams in uncomfortable ways in the early stages of team development.

"You are not only breaking your own rules, you are also failing to take action or hold each other accountable to them. If I weren't here, how would you normally proceed?"

Holding To Account

*A good ScrumMaster will
hold team members to account if needed.
A great ScrumMaster will hold the team to account
for not holding their teammates to account.*

During their efforts to tackle areas of waste in the National Health Service (NHS), researchers made an interesting discovery about the power of ownership. Cialdini discovered that General Practitioner (GP) offices could reduce the number of DNAs (did not attends / no-shows) by 18% simply by asking the patient to personally write down the appointment date instead having of the receptionist write it [5]. It turns out that patients are more likely to keep their commitments if they are actively involved in making them. The physical act of writing it had a material effect on them keeping their commitments. Cialdini attributes this to people's desire to act consistently with their view of themselves.

Scrum teams are no different. All groups operate under a set of explicit or implicit rules, what are often called working agreements. I've noticed that Scrum teams who write down their working agreements are much more likely to abide by and hold themselves accountable to them.

Take the Blue Peter team, for instance. Vince was facilitating his first sprint planning meeting as the new ScrumMaster of the Blue Peter team. The first thing Vince did was to ask the team what rules they normally have for these types of meetings, as he wanted to know how they would like to be facilitated. They responded with a number of statements including:

> *We start and finish on time*
> *Everybody's opinion should be heard*
> *There are no stupid ideas*
> *No electronic device distractions*
> *Make decisions by consensus*

Vince wrote the team's stated rules on a flipchart sheet, stuck it on the wall and began the meeting. Within 30 minutes, one of the team members, Janet, got her laptop out and started going through her inbox, replying to emails. The rest of the group looked at her, looked at the sheet on the wall, back at Janet and then at Vince, as if to say, "So what are you going to do about it?"

Vince considered for a moment. He was disappointed that Janet had shown disrespect to the team, the meeting, and her own commitment. He was more curious, though, as to why the rest of the team didn't feel able to pull Janet up on her behaviour.

Vince decided to ask the group about it. "Let's pause just a moment and return to our working agreements," he began. "Janet, I notice that you are on your computer right now. And I've noted a few times where one or two of you have interrupted each other. Both of these actions seem to violate the rules here on this flipchart," Vince concluded, pointing to the paper he'd hung on the wall.

"I'm sorry," Janet said quickly, blushing as she shut her laptop.

"My intention isn't to single you out, Janet," explained Vince. "You are not the only person who has violated the stated rules today, just the most recent. I want to ask the team a question: Are these agreements truly reflective of your intended behaviour? Because you are not only breaking your own rules, you are also failing to take action or hold each other accountable to them. If I weren't here, how would you normally proceed?"

The team members just looked at each other and shrugged.

Vince said, "Ultimately, you must be able to hold each other to account for your working agreements and feel responsible to each other for your behaviours. Let's talk about what would need to happen to make you comfortable doing that."

With Vince's help the team discussed why they created agreements but did not enforce them. They talked through obstacles to upholding what they all agreed were necessary rules, such as no electronic distractions. Janet explained that she felt compelled to check email often because managers expected an immediate response. Others agreed that this was a very real concern that made it hard to focus on meetings sometimes. The team felt that the rule of no electronic distractions still needed to be in place, but also put forth a few suggestions, such as regular email breaks and auto-responders, that they might use to help them stick to that commitment.

They also talked about the importance of allowing everyone the opportunity to speak, even if that meant holding a great idea back for a few more moments. In the end, they decided that the rules were not the problem; their failure to hold each other accountable to them was.

As the discussion wound down, the team agreed that Vince should walk them through the working agreements exercise again. This time Vince reminded the team to only include behaviours they really wanted to, and felt able to, commit to as a team. For each desired behaviour, Vince asked the team to describe its impact on the team.

For each proposed agreement the team voted on their level of support using their DECIDE™ cards [6] and, after some iterating and clarifying, anything that the team endorsed, defended or conceded was a rule they wanted to follow, one of the team members wrote it on the flipchart sheet. Vince ensured that everyone had the opportunity to personally write at least one rule. Once the rules were all on the sheet, the entire team signed it before hanging it in place of the original sheet on the wall.

First, Ask the Team

In his role as facilitator, Vince had a number of options when he noticed the team straying from their stated and posted working agreements. One response could have been to ignore it—after all, he was very new to the team. Another option would have been to question the team or to confront individual team members about why they were breaking rules they had posted only 30 minutes ago. In the specific case of Janet checking email, Vince could have shut Janet's laptop, or asked her to leave, although this could have been quite confrontational. Vince was within his rights as a facilitator to take a time-out to revisit the working agreement or alternatively could have asked the team if they needed a break to see to other responsibilities.

In this situation, Vince chose to point out the obvious—and less obvious—rule breaches he and others on the team had observed and ask the team what *they* planned to do about it. This was a very brave move by Vince. Letting this behaviour go, even just once, would have set a precedent that the team working agreements weren't that important. Solving the problem or confronting rule breakers would have taught the team that he would function as their rule police. Vince's decision to place the solution on the team's shoulders, while remaining non-judgemental, helped minimise defensive behaviour or a confrontation.

A good ScrumMaster would undoubtedly call people to account for breaking their commitments, no matter the situation. A ScrumMaster often plays the role of conscience of the team, especially when it is in the forming or norming stages of development [7]. Over time, however, the ScrumMaster should have the higher expectation that the team members will hold each other to account for failing to honour agreements.

Create A Feedback Culture

Giving honest feedback to someone who has broken faith with you is not an easy thing to do. Neither is accepting critical feedback from a peer. Teams will very likely need help in learning how to hold each other to account without inciting arguments or driving wedges between team members.

Scrum teams, the individuals within the teams, and the organisations they are operating in, all need to become comfortable with the process of giving and receiving feedback on a very frequent basis. We need to be open to feedback about the state of our requirements, our design decisions, our estimates, our priorities, our interactions with other team members, and, most importantly, what we have built and how we have built it.

Though many organisations *say* they value feedback—"It's the breakfast of champions" is a phrase I have heard many times—when it comes to it, people are either unskilled at, unprepared for, or unwilling to take good, proper, helpful feedback.

Ironically, those that think they are best at giving and receiving feedback are often the worst at it. A simple model to start off with is the AID model, which I came across in Max Landsberg's book, *The TAO of Coaching* [8]:

ACTIONS: What specifically is the person (or team) doing well, or poorly? Be objective where possible and focus on the behaviour not the individual(s).

IMPACTS: What effects are these actions having? Speak from your own perspective; not, for example, "I've heard that..." or "People have been saying..."

DESIRED OUTCOMES: What would good look like?

In the story, Vince noted that Janet's action (checking email during the meeting) had the impact of distracting others and diverted her attention from the meeting. Rather than blame Janet for breaking the rule, though, they worked together to come up with some ways (designated email breaks and auto-responders) to make it easier for them all to adhere to the rule and still be able to focus fully on the meeting.

There are other simple, yet effective models for giving feedback that a great ScrumMaster can introduce into the team to foster this practice. Sometimes, just focussing on the positive aspects of a behaviour, idea or delivery, and the ways it could be made even better is enough. One team that I was working with made a point of religiously using the phrase "What I like about that idea is…" This became such a motto for the team that they decided to change the name of their team to The WILATI'S. Another potential feedback tool is The Perfection Game, as described in the Core Protocols [9]. The Perfection Game effectively builds on the concept of WILATI by adding some constructive thoughts about how to extend the idea or behaviour in question.

I have found both of these models to be a good stepping-stone for helping teams get used to a feedback culture.

Scrum asks for organisations, teams and individuals to become comfortable with feedback on a more regular and tangible basis. This can be a shock for some and can take time to establish. All good ScrumMasters will find ways to provide the necessary feedback for all parties to make the decisions they need to make in order to be successful. Great ScrumMasters go one further and create the environment where feedback flows freely in all directions and becomes an accepted, expected and valued part of how we work.

RETRAINED

Enabling

"It is amazing what you can accomplish if you do not care who gets the credit."

Harry S. Truman

A ScrumMaster is much more of an enabler than a doer. ScrumMasters are there, first and foremost, to help people do what they need to do. Great ScrumMasters have a strong paternalistic streak—they enjoy helping their teams and the organisations they operate in develop and fulfill their potential.

Enablers take great pleasure in watching a team who were once accustomed to being told what to do and how to do it, start to take ownership of their work and deliver exceptional results into the bargain. It's also great to see customers take advantage of the opportunities available to them in Scrum and build extremely successful products very quickly.

It's even satisfying to facilitate a meeting in a way that fosters creativity, collaboration and commitment where previously there was tedium, tension and tacit disbelief.

TheFreeDictionary.com [1] describes the verb *enable* as:
1. To supply with the means, knowledge, or opportunity; make able.
2. To make feasible or possible

> **TIP** Find out what the team's biggest frustrations are in their work. Choose one that you could reduce or remove to increase their effectiveness.

In order to be a great enabler of a team, a ScrumMaster will need to remove impediments at both the team and organisational level. To remove impediments, ScrumMasters need to understand (or learn) how things get done in the organisation. Knowing whose door to knock on when an issue arises or what channels are most effective in gaining traction (and resolution) is often critical to a ScrumMaster's, and team's, success.

> **TIP** Try "battle mapping" [2] to map out both the formal and informal structures of your organisation, interactions, power relationships and spheres of influence.

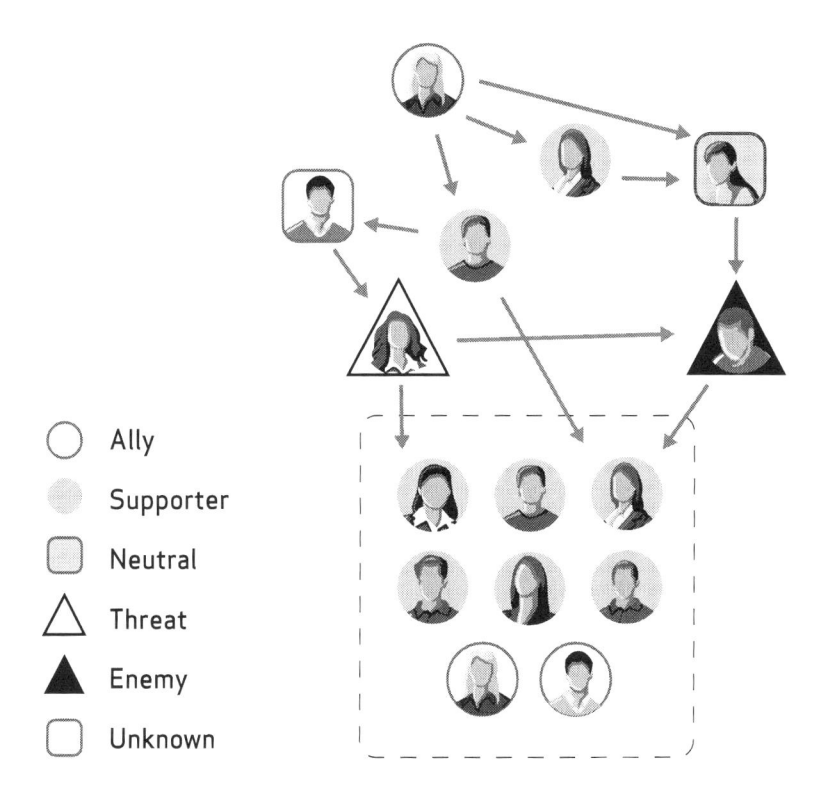

- ○ Ally
- ● Supporter
- ▢ Neutral
- △ Threat
- ▲ Enemy
- ◯ Unknown

As well as this positive definition of the verb to enable, there is another, less positive definition on the very same page:

To behave in a manner that facilitates or supports another's abusive, addictive, or self-destructive behaviour.

The desire to "rescue" your people or "make things easier" for them is noble and positive. A problem that many ScrumMasters face is that rescuing can be addictive too and sometimes rescuing the team increases the dependency upon the ScrumMaster rather than increasing the team's autonomy and agency. This is also known as The White Knight Syndrome [3].

ScrumMasters need to develop their skills at the positive form of enabling without falling into the traps of the negative forms of enabling.

Enabling

*"BUZZZZZ....Come on Fin,
you can do better than that, can't you?"*

The Bulls**t Buzzer

*A good ScrumMaster is wary of influencing the team.
A great ScrumMaster can act normally and know the team
will still make their own decisions*

ScrumMasters often have to exercise judicious caution about what to say, when to say it and how to say it for fear of influencing someone's behaviour, leading them to a particular decision or putting them on the spot and discouraging further involvement. That's why the best Scrum teams keep each other in check, rather than depending on the Scrum-Master to do it for them.

One tool I've seen teams use to hold each other accountable during a daily scrum is a buzzer. At any time, if a speaker is being too vague, too detailed, using jargon, or generally not giving the team the information it needs, any one of their team-mates will activate the buzzer to bring the speaker back on track. But be careful, if you're the ScrumMaster and do your job right, some day the person that gets buzzed might just be you.

Take The Divas for example. The Divas team were having their daily scrum. Their ScrumMaster, Fin, took his turn to update the team on the progress that he had made on one of the team's impediments.

"Well yesterday," began Fin. "You said you were having an issue with not being able to get in touch with the vendor so I put out a few emails and I left a voicemail with…"
"BUZZZZZZZZ"

Jaime had pushed the "bulls**t buzzer" to interrupt the ScrumMaster mid-sentence.

"What?" asked Fin.

"Emails and voicemail? Really? Come on, Fin, you can do better than that, can't you?" asked Jaime.

"Fair point, Jaime. I was a bit busy yesterday and so took the easy option. I meant to follow up in the afternoon but got sidetracked," Fin admitted. "Good call. So that was yesterday. Obviously, today I'm going to get an answer about the config details from the vendor. If necessary, I'll drive over there."

It was then Theo's turn. Theo was a new member of the Divas. Fin thought Theo seemed a little shy, especially in the daily scrum, so he was keeping an eye on him to make sure he was OK. Fin remembered that it's sometimes hard to join an established team, especially one that is going along quite nicely.

Theo stated that, after learning about the storage parameters yesterday, today he was going to "find out about the upload facility."

Fin's curiosity was sparked by Theo's comments. They seemed a little vague and non-committal. He wanted to ask Theo about them in a little more detail but was worried how he might react if questioned in front of the whole team, so Fin waited until after the daily scrum had finished before asking Theo for a quick chat.

"How are you settling in, Theo?" Fin asked.

"Not bad. There's a lot to learn but it's all interesting."

"You mentioned that you were going to look into the upload facility today. Is there anything I can help with in that regard?"

"Not really," Theo explained. "It's just a case of finding stuff out. I know it wouldn't take the rest of the guys very long but I'm still getting up to speed with things really. To be honest I was half expecting to get the bulls**t buzzer treatment but perhaps they are cutting me a little slack."

"So how about pairing up with one of the others? Would that help you out?" asked Fin.

"Well obviously yes but I don't want to slow the team down even more," explained Theo.

"You won't," said Fin. "Pairing to help each other learn and get new members up to speed is what we do."

"You know," admitted Theo. "I was a bit afraid of the buzzer until I saw Jaime use it on you. At my last company, the agile project manager acted like he wanted to hear what was going on, but if you told the truth about anything you were struggling with, he tended to report it to management or use it against you later. I figure if the team is holding your feet to the fire about your updates, it can't be like that here."

"Wow I can see why that would affect you Theo, but no, the Divas aren't giving me a status report. We're sharing with each other. Never be afraid to ask for help. And don't think you can avoid the buzzer forever. You can see, they're pretty ruthless," Fin added, smiling.

Creating a Trusting Team

The Divas were a well-established team with a relatively informal and frank approach to managing themselves—the bulls**t buzzer. On the day I watched this particular daily scrum, it was particularly refreshing to see a team member buzz the ScrumMaster, as it demonstrated that there was no sense of authority or standing on ceremony with regards to the team's ScrumMaster.

Another sign that the Divas were a healthy team was that they and their ScrumMaster recognised that a new team member might not be ready for the buzzer treatment yet. Knowing when to speak up and when to wait is a skill that the best ScrumMasters cultivate. Though Fin (and likely the rest of the team) noticed that Theo was vague in his comments, Fin chose to speak to Theo privately instead of buzzing him or questioning him publicly.

As Fin noted, it can be difficult to join a well-established team. When a new team member joins, it may even be worth revisiting the team norms and practices to see if there are existing customs that might seem odd, be inappropriate, or require explanation. Always remember that what is simple fun and banter with one set of people may not have the same effect when the composition of the team changes.

New team members often benefit from pairing with different members of the team. It helps decrease their learning curve and builds relationships. When assimilating a new team member, you might also focus daily scrum updates on a product backlog item at a time rather than one person at a time, thus reducing the focus on any one member and increasing the focus on the work.

By re-examining team norms, establishing a pairing rotation, and focusing on the work during daily scrums, new team members will assimilate much more quickly. Soon the team will return to a state where they will all be able to act completely normally in the face of anything that their ScrumMaster says or does.

A team that feels comfortable with each other and their ScrumMaster has the potential to reach a truly high-performing state. When the ScrumMaster can challenge the team, and each individual, with some really powerful questions and observations that the team can take on face value, the team can use them as valuable reflection points for equally powerful growth.

*"Whoa. What's that?"
asked Phillip.
"That's not what I asked for!"*

The Problem With Proxies

*A good ScrumMaster will ensure
the team have access to a product owner.
A great ScrumMaster will ensure the team
have access to **the** product owner.*

"Scrum would be fine if only we had a product owner!" I have heard this from many teams who are frustrated because they don't have a product owner, they have the wrong product owner, or they have the right product owner and either can't communicate effectively or just never get to see or speak to them.

Take the Oscars team for example. They had a product owner, Phillip, but did not have much access to him during the sprint. Phillip was a former business analyst who was used to handing off requirements documents. The team had tried to reach him for questions during past sprints but he had put them off, telling them that everything they needed to know was in the user story and that he could answer questions during the sprint review. This lack of communication came to a head during one sprint review when team member Jimmy was demonstrating the new migration functionality.

"Whoa. What's that?" asked Phillip "That's not what I asked for!"

"What do you mean?" replied Jimmy, quite shocked. "Look at the story. It specifically says we should migrate the active users to the new system."

"Well, sure, technically it meets what the requirement said but it's missed the point of what I was after," said Phillip. "I only wanted to migrate the users in groups A-D to this type of account. Users in the other groups should have been migrated to the secondary account."

"Well, that's not our fault," said Jimmy defensively. "We couldn't ask you about it during the sprint, so we just followed the story to the letter. "

Frank, the ScrumMaster, suggested the team take this up in the retrospective after the review to see if the team could work out what happened and how to avoid it in the future.

"Should we roll back this feature, Phillip? Or would you like it to stay and then we can separate out the two account types next sprint?" Frank asked.

"We can't deploy this feature like this so we will have to roll it back," Phillip confirmed.

During the sprint retrospective, the first item the team discussed was the lack of access to Phillip during the sprint. Philip explained that while he'd like to help the team better understand his needs, he just couldn't free up enough time to answer all of their questions. Frank suggested that they try a proxy product owner.

"A proxy is empowered to explain your requirements and answer questions on your behalf," he explained. "But understand that if we build something according to the way the proxy describes it, and it still doesn't match your true requirements, that's something you'll need to take up with the proxy. We have to go by what the proxy says if you aren't here."

Phillip agreed to find someone to act as proxy. Unfortunately, despite having a proxy, there were still misunderstandings that surfaced at the sprint review at the end of the next sprint.

Frank was prepared for this eventuality and came to the next sprint retrospective with a breakdown of the cost of Phillip being unavailable during the sprint.

	Time Spent Waiting for Answers	Time Spent Redoing "Wrong" Work	Total Time	Daily Rate	Cost of Proxy
SPRINT 1	2 days	8 days	10 days	£900	£9,000
SPRINT 2	1 day	7 days	8 days	£900	£7,200
SPRINT 3	2 days	5 days	7 days	£900	£6,300
			Total Cost		£22,500
			Annualised Cost		£90,000

"I've broken down our costs in terms of wasted effort, unnecessary re-work, time spent waiting for decisions to be made, and so on. By totalling the number of hours or days and multiplying by the daily cost of the Scrum team, you can see we have a pretty viable business case for freeing up your time. Not having a product owner that is available during the sprint, even when we use a proxy, has a real, measurable cost."

Frank and Phillip took this information to the management team and convinced them to rethink the idea of a proxy. They decided to free up some of Phillip's time during the sprint by bringing in someone to help

Phillip with testing and product backlog management. This proxy helped with the elements of Phillip's job that were much easier to delegate and left the task of interacting with the team to Phillip himself.

As Phillip worked more closely with the team during the sprint, not only did the team begin to create the features Phillip actually wanted, but Phillip and the team also began to like and trust each other, fostering creative solutions that neither could have come up with alone.

Encouraging Customer Collaboration

Product owners have many different perspectives to consider, both within the organisation and outside it. As such, they can easily get overloaded. Many, like Phillip, manage to find time to ensure that the product backlog is prioritised and sized appropriately enough for the sprint planning sessions and attend every sprint review meeting. But too often, they are unavailable during the sprint itself. This leaves teams to make a number of assumptions about the requirements in an attempt to implement them.

The agile manifesto talks about valuing customer collaboration over contract negotiation; the product owner role is an attempt to bring conversation into the sprint rather than rely on written instructions. ScrumMasters must ensure that the team get the answers they need during the sprint, which typically involves working with the product owner to improve product backlog items, facilitating better relationships, and removing impediments that stand in the way of team access to the product owner. Let's examine some of the ways ScrumMasters can help reduce the distance between the team and the product owner.

User Stories & Acceptance Criteria

When product owners are unavailable during the sprint, most teams try tighter requirements or delegation. Ironically, user stories [4] are the choice for most teams who are looking to move *away* from tightly defined, up-front requirements. The underlying problem of product owner access is not going to be resolved by user stories because user stories are quite openly a token (or placeholder) for a conversation. They are not a contract for a feature and can only really work if followed up with a conversation about the need expressed in the story.

Proxies

Teams that lack access to a product owner are forced to rely too much on the card that the requirement, or user story, is written on and not enough on the conversation. One way to mitigate this is to delegate user story elaboration to a proxy. A proxy is somebody who represents the product owner on a day-to-day basis during the sprint and is empowered to make decisions on the product owner's behalf. Even the most trusted and knowledgeable proxies still don't always understand exactly what the product owner wants, but they are a bridge for a team that cannot get product owner time any other way.

Though proxies are better than no product owner access at all, they are far from ideal. Assigning a proxy fails to tackle the real problem of why a product owner is too busy to interact with the team. Is the product owner working on too many pieces of work? Does the product owner not have the support of an adequate product owner team? Is the product owner spending too much time with the stakeholders or identifying more product backlog items (or user stories) than the team can deal with? Is the product owner testing or creating bug reports from the previous sprint?

Ideally proxies, if used at all, should be dealing with these elements of the product owner workload rather than the interface with the developers.

The product owner is a crucial role in Scrum. Great ScrumMasters avoid putting sticking plasters or Band Aids over the problem and work instead to resolve the real issue—in this case helping free enough time for the product owner to spend time talking to the team during the sprint. Showcasing the true costs of creating features that have to be rolled back and rebuilt because the team did not understand all of the requirements can help make it easier for a product owner to justify dedicating time to the team during the sprint.

Only True Product Owners Will Do

Good ScrumMasters will do everything possible to bridge the gap between the product owner and the developers so that they build the right product in the right way. ScrumMasters should be prepared to do whatever is needed to facilitate an effective working relationship between these two parties. Great ScrumMasters realise, however, that being the go-between, arbiter or the translator is not the optimal long-term strategy.

As the agile manifesto states: "Business people and developers must work together daily throughout the project."

Great ScrumMasters know that ultimately they need to do whatever it takes *not* to function as a go-between. Instead they should aim to bring the team and product owner together so that they work hand-in-hand (not literally though, that would be a little weird).

For more information on how to become, or coach, a great Product Owner check out my book Product Mastery: From Good to Great Product Ownership [5].

*"Business people and developers must
work together daily throughout the project."*

Holly shut down Zoom, closed the laptop and rolled her head round, clicking her neck.

Be Selfish to Be Generous

A Good ScrumMaster Serves Others
A Great ScrumMaster Serves Themselves
So They Can Serve Others

"Thanks so much for your help, Holly. Having you as a ScrumMaster is one of my favourite things about our team sometimes," said Charlie "I'm sorry I kept you so late. I hope I haven't ruined your evening."

"No problem, Charlie. That's my job. I'm glad to help and you know I'm always here if you need me," replied Holly. "Hopefully you can relax now and enjoy your weekend. I'll see you on Monday."

Holly shut down Zoom, closed the laptop and rolled her head round, clicking her neck. She suddenly realised she had a throbbing headache and that she'd been sitting in the same position for over three hours without a break. She looked at the clock. 7:15pm. "I'm going to be in trouble again!" she thought to herself as she made her way downstairs from the spare room, now doubling as the home office.

As she entered the kitchen her partner Morgan handed her a glass of wine asking, "Another tough day, babe?"

"Yes and no," Holly replied. "The team have been really struggling lately and I feel I've finally been able to help a couple of them. Charlie especially seems in a much better place now."

The team had indeed been under a lot of pressure recently. Some regulatory changes had come out of nowhere a week ago, causing a mad scramble to incorporate them into the current sprint. Unfortunately, the sprint was already full with work on a highly visible commitment for an important customer. The team had felt they had no choice but to focus on both priorities but were struggling to make it all happen.

Plus, since the team had all been working remote lately, Holly had observed that they had been finding it harder to collaborate and communicate. It seemed that they were constantly running to her telling tales rather than working things out themselves. Holly made a mental note to organise a bit of remote pairing next week and possibly a virtual team building event to bring morale and collaboration back up a bit.

"You haven't heard a word I just said, have you?" laughed Morgan.

"Uh..um.." said Holly, as she racked her brains trying to recall anything Morgan had said that she might have registered subconsciously. It was no use.

"Sorry…I guess I still haven't switched off." Holly conceded.

"I'm a bit worried about you, H. You seem to be taking far too much responsibility for what's happening, like it's all up to you to make sure it all works out." Morgan said.

"We've just got to get through this next month or two and then things will settle down again."

"I think I've heard that before." Morgan teased.

"Yeah…I know." Holly conceded. "Wait a minute. What do you mean I'm taking too much responsibility?" she asked.

"Well, it seems like everyone comes to you with their problems and you feel it's up to you to find a solution for them. What are others doing to help find solutions?" Morgan asked gently.

"Hmmm…" Holly thought, then said "Do you know what? I think you're right," and let out what sounded like a growl before smacking herself round the head.

"What's up?" Morgan asked.

"I've just realised I've been making things worse."

"What do you mean? You've been *helping* people!"

"Yes, but I've been taking the quick option, the easy option. I've been advising, telling and solving people's problems rather than asking, coaching and helping them to identify and solve their own problems." Holly said.

Morgan considered for a moment, then said, "I know you can't talk to *me* about the details because of confidentiality but do you have anyone you can share the load with? I don't want this rattling around in your head and you beating yourself up over it."

"Yeah…good call, let me just make a note to speak to Sam about it on Monday and then I'll be able to let it go for the weekend."

Holly had a bit of history with negative self-talk, berating herself internally for what she believed to be mistakes she had made. Morgan had seen it often enough to be able to help Holly catch herself when it started. Holly had also developed a few techniques, such as writing her thoughts down and talking them through with people, to nip it in the bud.

Sam was another Scrum Master at Holly's company and they regularly talked to each other about the challenges they came across in their role. On Monday, Holly spoke to Sam about her concerns.

"I think I've been taking shortcuts with the team recently because I've been under a bit of pressure. I didn't realise it until I was talking to Morgan about it." Holly explained.

"I'm not surprised. With the recent demands, your team have been under tremendous pressure lately. I think most people in your position would have buckled by now." Replied Sam. "Has there been any cost to keeping the team going so well for so long?"

Holly thought for a few seconds before replying, "Well, I'm lucky that Morgan has been so understanding and supportive; I've probably run the risk of putting work ahead of that relationship."

"You did mention feeling guilty about that and joking about being in trouble again," Sam replied. "If this were another ScrumMaster, what would your advice be to them?" Sam asked.

"Oh…you're good!" Holly said before taking a good couple of minutes to think. She then started thinking out loud, "I would probably tell them to be proud of helping the team continue to meet their goals in really challenging times, but I would also be talking to them about falling into playing the White Knight."

Holly and Sam had talked about her previous struggles with White Knight Syndrome [3] before. It's a problem common to those in helping professions, such as medicine, therapy, teaching and servant-leadership. It referred to the subconscious desire to continue rescuing those the helper is helping. While ostensibly a positive driver, it had the negative consequence of undermining the helper's ability and willingness to get those they were helping to a level of self-sufficiency, for fear the helper would no longer be needed.

"And if that ScrumMaster were playing the role of rescuer, which would be understandable given the pressures and their commitment to the team, what would your advice be to them?"

"I would probably recommend taking a break," Holly said, "but I can't take time off now. It would be the worst time to abandon the team."

"Interesting choice of word. Is it really *abandoning* them?" questioned Sam.

"It shouldn't make me feel that way, should it? You've given me a lot to consider. Once this hump is over, I'm definitely getting away for a break. I think the finish line is in sight," Holly said. "Thanks for listening, Sam, just talking about it was a help."

The next day was Tuesday, Holly's birthday. At the end of the morning's daily scrum, Lou posted a link in the chat window and asked Holly to click it. It was a digital birthday card from the team.

Holly blushed as she read the card and her eyes widened when she saw what was written.

"You guys!" said Holly. "You really shouldn't have. I haven't had a spa break for ages – it's amazing. Thank you so much!"

"There are just two problems," said Lou. "You have to take the break on two consecutive weekdays and it has to be before the end of the month."

"But it's already the 23rd!" said Holly.

"Exactly!" said Lou. "Don't take this the wrong way but we figured you really need a break!"

Holly's story is an all too common one for ScrumMasters around the world. It's so difficult sometimes to see when our efforts to help the team are actually going too far and achieving almost the opposite of our intention.

A common cause of this, exemplified by Holly here, is working at a personally unsustainable pace. Telling people what to do is always going to be quicker than helping someone reflect, self-analyse and find their own solution. When pushed for time because we have taken on too much, it is almost inevitable that we will revert to the quicker option. Unfortunately, this typically only increases the unsustainable pace for the helper as they become the bottleneck.

Time pressure is one common reason for taking the shorter, more directive approach to helping a team, but the other is the desire to rescue that comes from an overblown people-pleaser driver, resulting in the White Knight Syndrome. This can be difficult to spot in oneself so it was great that Holly had Sam to talk to.

You may have noticed Sam modeled the more reflective practice of asking Holly questions to address the situation and also encouraged her to adopt an alternative perspective, viewing her situation as if it were someone else, making things like her rescuer tendencies easier to spot.

People also take shortcuts when they are tired. Holly needed a break, something she would have recognised in others but couldn't see in herself. As it turned out, the team noticed it as well and, far from feeling abandoned, they actually took the opportunity to dial up their self-management and empowerment. When Holly returned from her time off, the team had stepped up in many ways that they simply wouldn't had Holly stuck around in her rescuer and protector persona.

One issue I have found with ScrumMasters is that they often find it very hard to ask for help, even though they are regularly telling others that they need to ask for help! There are many reasons for this: Perhaps they want to appear strong, perhaps they fear they may lose face or people's respect. One common underlying reason is they don't want to be a burden to others.

This is interesting, because when I ask ScrumMasters whether they feel other people are a burden when they ask for help, they typically say no. They enjoy the opportunity to help other people. So I tend to ask them why they would deny other people the chance to feel good by helping them. I like to say:

Be generous and ask for help.
Be selfish and offer it.

Robert Greenleaf wrote many years ago, in his essay on Servant Leadership:

"the art of withdrawal is useful. …The ability to withdraw and reorient oneself, if only for a moment, presumes that one has learned the art of systematic neglect to sort out the more important from the less important – and the important from the urgent – and attend to the more important… Pacing oneself by appropriate withdrawal is one of the best approaches to making optimal use of one's resources"

The analogy I tend to refer to is similar to that which you hear on airplanes, that a great ScrumMaster will fit their own oxygen mask before helping others. Not because they are selfish but because they are no use to anyone if they have no oxygen.

In addition to taking breaks, ScrumMasters can practice many forms of withdrawal. What rejuvenates and provokes reflection for each person will be different, so be prepared to experiment. Perhaps try shutting everything off for an hour and just be unavailable. Take walks, eat lunch away from messaging apps and email. This can be especially helpful when you're remote or working from home, where the lines between work and home life can become increasingly blurred.

Since the role was invented, there has been a growing number of Scrum-Masters who have found tremendous value in the practice of supervision – either informally as Holly and Sam did in the story – or more explicitly engaging with another coach or supervisor to guide their own reflection. Indeed, can one really ethically advocate for others to self-reflect if one isn't practicing self-reflection oneself? Would you visit a dentist who didn't practice good dental hygiene?

Keeping a journal is another effective way of consciously and mindfully reflecting on one's practice that I have seen in ScrumMasters I have worked with. Debriefing each day in a ritualistic manner helps avoid the build-up of unconscious behaviours.

Whatever way you can, ensure that you are practicing what you preach and avoiding burning out. Be a little selfish so that you can keep yourself in optimum condition to role model desirable behaviours.

RETRAINED

Tactful

"A dead ScrumMaster is a useless ScrumMaster."

Ken Schwaber [1]

ScrumMasters are expected to embody the Scrum principle of *The Art Of The Possible* – making the best of each and every situation in order to move the team and the organisation forward. They are also, however, expected to be ruthlessly determined to push their teams and organisations towards a new state of teamwork, organisation and performance. Transforming a team, let alone an entire organisation, from the principles of command and control to those based on servant-leadership, from plans based on prediction to plans based on empirical, evolutionary data requires both patience and tenacity. To remove the impediments to team productivity and then resolve the organisational issues in order to facilitate the painfully slow transformation to a more agile organisation requires determination and resilience.

It can be very easy to give up, thinking, "This organisation will never change" or "This team just isn't stepping up to the plate in terms of self-management," so it is very important to regularly reflect and keep a tally of progress and achievements both at the team and the organisation level

> **TIP** Note signs of progress, even if they are little things like "John felt able to join in the retrospective" or "People are looking at each other in the daily scrum rather than their feet" or "Dave offered to help Arush today without anyone prompting him." These small details may get lost in the bigger picture but can serve as energy reserves when things don't seem to be progressing as fast as you would like

While being effective in the ScrumMaster role will require you to be tenacious, controversial and resourceful to the point of bending or breaking rules, it's equally important to be tactful. Great ScrumMasters, while impatient for success and change, are sensitive to each situation they face, considerate of the people involved and the consequences of every action.

They will consciously ruffle some feathers, stand up for what is right and, to some extent, deliberately provoke difficult conversations. However they will do so with care and respect for the fact that current processes and behaviours were always rational at some point and that they have an element of emotional attachment for people. Great ScrumMasters are not loose cannons constantly railing against their organisations. They pick their confrontations carefully and are prepared to accept certain compromises in order to have the opportunity to continue the battle another day.

> **TIP** Practice staying calm (the old adage of counting to ten never gets old) when confronting a challenge. Take your time before sending emails or making phone calls. If you can, run through your views and arguments with a colleague before presenting them to your actual audience. Use the feedback to gauge just how provocative your message and tone is.

*"Annika would freak
if she saw the real sprint burndown!"*

A Tale Of Two Scrums

A good ScrumMaster removes disruptive influences from the daily scrum so it is used for the team's benefit. A great ScrumMaster will create an environment where others (particularly the product owner) can attend and not affect the behaviour of the team.

The sprint burndown and the daily scrum are two of the Scrum tools available to the team to allow them to effectively manage themselves during a sprint. They are not, as some people think, reporting tools for management (or anyone else) to check on the progress of the team on a daily basis.

Good ScrumMasters will create a safe environment where the team feel able to share their progress, ideas and concerns with each other. Great ScrumMasters will create that environment and then push the boundaries such that the team are comfortable involving the product owner (and everyone else) in activities like the daily scrum.

One experience in particular brought this fact into sharp relief for me. It was first thing in the morning on my first day coaching a new team, Team Icarus, who had invited me along to their daily scrum. They had been using Scrum for a couple of months and had commandeered a great meeting room with glass walls on all sides and a lovely view of the lake. On one wall they had their sprint backlog, on another they had the sprint burndown, and on another they had the outcomes from the last retrospective.

Everybody was there on time. Even Annika, the product owner, was demonstrating her commitment to the team by being present. There were a few quick greetings before the team members stood in a circle and took turns to update their colleagues on their progress, confirming the view indicated by the sprint burndown that they were making good progress towards their sprint goal. The daily scrum didn't last too long, probably only about six or seven minutes, before the team dispersed, preferring to get back to work.

I was pleased. Rarely am I called in to coach a team that is progressing so well. On my way back to the team room, I was already contemplating all of the advanced topics I could cover with such an evolved team. No sooner had we gotten back to the space where the team worked, however, than I saw Stephanie, the ScrumMaster, look furtively around. I then watched as she grabbed another printed copy of the sprint burndown out of a drawer. The team gathered around her and then proceeded to have another daily scrum.

This daily scrum was much different from the one I had just witnessed. The new sprint burndown implied the team were *not* on track to meet their sprint goal. When I asked what was going on, Stephanie told me, "This is the *real* daily scrum; the first one was just for the product owner. Annika would freak if she saw the real sprint burndown!"

I held my shock in check and said, "Interesting. I gather she has not reacted well to past burndowns?"

"Yes," confirmed one of the team members. "The last time we showed her a sprint burndown that was trending badly, she decided that she wasn't being hands-on enough. She was constantly checking up on us, interrupting our work every five minutes to ask us how we were doing and asking us to stay late until we were back on track!"

"Exactly," confirmed Stephanie. "So you can see why we have to have two daily scrums. The team are confident that they are on track and things are under control but the sprint burndown is not doing us justice. It takes less than 10 minutes a day to tell Annika what she wants to hear, and then she's out of our way until the review."

Always Err on the Side of Agile Values

Sometimes ScrumMasters may choose to deliberately break rules that seem to fly in the face of agile principles. Stephanie and the team certainly were breaking the rules, but not for the right reasons.

I can see how Stephanie might have felt justified in her actions. The Scrum-Master has a responsibility to protect the team and allow them to be productive as they focus on achieving their sprint goal in the best way they can. If anyone is distracting the team, putting them under unnecessary pressure or stealing their focus then the ScrumMaster should try to reduce or remove this. However, the ScrumMaster also has a responsibility to foster relationships between the product owner and the developers, to promote transparency, trust and a sense of "one team." By deceiving the product owner or hiding the truth, a ScrumMaster runs the risk of driving a wedge between the product owner and the rest of the Scrum team, decreasing the trust the product owner has in the team and the process.

Ironically, by shielding the team from the product owner's scrutiny, Scrum-Masters also can inadvertently make it harder to remove the impediments that stand in the way of their teams' success. The best product owners get involved in helping the team remove the impediments, and are often rewarded with an instant improvement in the velocity of their team. Even though impediment removal is officially the responsibility of the ScrumMaster, the product owner is typically from another part of the organisation, with a different network and sphere of influence, and can work with the ScrumMaster to be doubly effective at enabling the team to be productive. This can only happen, however, if there is visibility.

In the story of Annika and Stephanie, the fact that the ScrumMaster and developers felt the need to put on a charade for the product owner was definitely not a good sign about the health of the relationships in the Scrum team. Great ScrumMasters learn to expose such issues by talking openly with the product owner and by taking the whole team further down the path of discovery to find a better solution-one that is more aligned with the agile values of transparency and collaboration.

Create a Safe Environment

Having an audience at daily scrums and retrospectives can be uncomfortable for developers. Some of the worst daily scrums and retrospectives I have seen have had product owners present. Oddly enough though, some of the best daily scrums I have seen also have product owners present. This goes to show that while product owner involvement in daily scrums (and retrospectives for that matter) can be a destructive thing if handled badly, it can be highly productive if handled well.

In the early stages of team development, ScrumMasters should help establish trust and safety for the team. Jean Tabaka suggests that collaborative leaders "take away the blame" by helping shift conversations away from finding blame towards finding solutions and, if necessary, shouldering any blame yourself. By doing this "the team learns that taking ownership is possible without suffering the destruction of blame." [2]

Establishing some explicit rules for the formal meetings, such as *nothing said here leaves this room*, can also help foster a more transparent environment. Try starting the daily scrum (or retrospective) with a short confessions session, where everyone (even neutral observers) shares a short example of something they screwed up. This can increase the shared level of vulnerability and the sense that not everything always goes to plan.

Creating a process of gradual exposure is also a common pattern that great ScrumMasters tend to follow. Daily scrums and retrospectives start off as behind-closed-doors or off-site meetings. As the team grows comfortable with each other, they can extend an invitation to the product owner—perhaps for a safe meeting first—and, then gradually for meetings where the team has a higher risk of exposure. I would recommend an element of priming the product owner (or any other stakeholder) for how to avoid negatively influencing the team's behaviour.

Working up to a level of trust will help teams feel less anxious about their visibility and prevent them from losing value in the meetings altogether. Remember that while protecting the team by excluding disruptive influences may be a good short-term strategy, great ScrumMasters work towards a more inclusive and transparent process. Eventually your team should reach a point where the product owner—as well as any other stakeholder—is included in team meetings, such as the daily scrum.

*"I can see things don't look good
and I really appreciate the fact that you are all
being very open about where we are."*

How Long Is a Piece Of String?

A good ScrumMaster will help a team change their sprint length to find their optimum. A great ScrumMaster has faith in self-management and knows the value of rhythm

The debate over sprint lengths has been around as long as Scrum itself. In the early days of Scrum, there was (officially at least) no argument; sprints were 30 calendar days long. Over time, however, teams have experimented with different iteration timeboxes. This is a good thing.

One of my clients went through a typical sprint length debate. As the Tempura Team was entering the final week of their sprint, they began to question whether their sprint was the right length.

"…so I've made some progress but there's no way I'm going to be finished with my other tasks by the end of the week," said Maya

"Same here I'm afraid," added Bo. "We need more time, Robin."

Robin, the ScrumMaster, looked at the outstanding tasks and the burndown chart that was showing they were behind schedule. It was clear the sprint commitment was in jeopardy.

"OK. I can see things don't look good and I really appreciate the fact that you are all being very open about where we are. However, I'm not convinced that extending the sprint is the solution."

"What do you mean?" asked Bo. "We probably only need a few more days."

"An extra week, tops," added Maya.

Robin thought for a second and said, "I believe you. And I really think it would be a good idea to have a look at our sprint length at the end of the sprint—but I don't want us to extend this sprint. For now, though, I think we should do what we can to finish as many of the outstanding items as possible by the original sprint deadline. Tell me what you think is achievable and what is at risk and I will break the news to [the product owner] Alex."

The team re-organised their sprint backlog and ended up dropping three features from the sprint. When Robin brought this up in the retrospective, the team were still disappointed at not being allowed to finish them by extending the deadline a bit.

"I still don't understand why we couldn't just have had an extra week to complete everything," Maya said. "I think that six-week sprints are probably more appropriate for us going forward."

"Fair enough," Robin said. "I did say we would consider changing the sprint length at the end of this sprint so let's do that. I'd like you to break up into groups of two or three people and list out what you think we could gain from having a longer sprint and also what you think we could gain from a shorter sprint, say two weeks long."

After ten minutes the groups came back and Robin collated all the pros and cons of longer and shorter sprints

"It looks as though longer sprints would allow us to complete more work and have less incomplete pieces of work that have to carry over into the next sprint. Oh, and they would be less stressful," he summarized. "It appears that shorter sprints are more focussed and would give us more opportunities to get feedback and make changes."

"Can I just jump in here?" asked Alex. "I don't think we have the option of longer sprints because we have a release in two months."

"Good point. Let's try a slightly different angle here," suggested Robin. "What would make you more comfortable with shorter sprints?"

"Smaller pieces of work would help," said Bo, jumping into the conversation. "Some of these product backlog items are quite big and quite vague."

"That's true," agreed Maya. "And if we could speed up some of our manual processes that would help. We've got a big overhead there."

"Personally I think it would be an interesting experiment to run a two-week sprint to see how it feels," said Robin.

Nobody looked very keen. Maya said, "I'm not sure about going to two weeks but, if we got smaller user stories and some time to automate then I think we would be better able to cope with four-week sprints."

"OK. Let's do a *fist of five [2]* on that suggestion then." suggested Robin.

The team all voted by displaying the number of fingers that indicated their level of support for the suggestion and, given that everyone had at least three fingers of support, the team decided to adopt it.

Parkinson's Law [3]

Cyril Northcote Parkinson once said that "Work expands so as to fill the time available for its completion" and this has been hailed as a humourous truism ever since. The agile manifesto recommends an iteration length of "a couple of weeks to a couple of months, with a preference to the shorter timescale. [4]" Shorter sprints do allow for greater risk reduction, earlier feedback and more opportunities to adapt to change.

Longer sprints, however, offer more breathing space for the team and can therefore allow for greater creativity within the sprint as well as increase the chances of things being completed. It's a difficult balance for teams to strike.

What teams should *never* do, however, is extend the sprint, not even by just a couple of days. The rhythm of delivery is far too important to compromise and it is a terrible precedent to set.

Balancing Pace & Rhythm

Maintaining a sustainable pace is key to Scrum teams. The optimal sprint length will balance getting things done and being adaptable to change with a pace that can be sustained indefinitely without physical or mental burnout or resorting to cutting quality. In general, teams develop more quickly and become more predictable if they keep a constant sprint length. They learn what they are capable of delivering within a given timebox and optimise their working practices to deliver their best within the time available. Therefore, you could argue that a good ScrumMaster would help the team find the right rhythm and keep it.

Great ScrumMasters know that the length of the sprint is rarely the true problem and so encourage the team to stick with their chosen sprint length even when it's hard. If teams maintain one sprint length for a few sprints, resisting the temptation to extend it to ease the pressure, they will soon normalise to the timebox and find ways to work effectively within it.

In the story, Robin was very careful not to impose a solution on the team. He asked them to consider the pros and cons of different sprint lengths, including shorter ones, and encouraged them to discuss what would help them work inside the timebox. He also made good use of a consensus-building tool to ensure the team were comfortable with the decision they made to stick with their current sprint length.

In general I typically recommend teams start off with shorter sprints. Once they have optimised their processes and established a predictable velocity, they can then consider extending it to take advantage of the greater focus that a longer sprint offers.

"So did you deliberately turn up late this morning to see how we would handle it?"

The Power of Silence

A good ScrumMaster will say what needs to be said.
A great ScrumMaster knows the power of silence.

Early in the book, in the chapter "Above All, Empower the Team," I told you that ScrumMasters should first ask the team and then try to make themselves redundant. Both of these facets of the role are evident in the following story of Ossie, a ScrumMaster who was trying to help the team take greater control of their own process and become more self-managing.

Ossie looked at his watch. 8:52. The daily scrum was scheduled to have started 7 minutes ago. Curious as to whether it had begun without him, he stood up, picked up his coffee and wandered over to the Shandies' Scrum room. There was a mixture of relief, frustration and concern on the faces of the team as he wandered in.

"Where have you been?" asked Ricky.

"Don't worry about me," Ossie replied. "I'm more interested in what you guys have been doing"

"What do you mean?"

"Well, what have I missed?"

"Nothing yet, we were waiting for you," explained a somewhat confused Ricky.

"Why would you do that?" asked Ossie.

"Ummm…because this is the daily scrum…and you're the ScrumMaster?" offered Ricky.

"Interesting," began Ossie. "I've had a feeling recently that something wasn't quite right in these meetings, like it all revolved about me. Is that what you think?"

"Not exactly," joined in Perry. "But you are supposed to facilitate them, right?"

"Fair point, Perry. So how does me being late count as facilitation?" asked Ossie.

"Well, it's the exact opposite. You are specifically *not* facilitating the meeting," replied Ricky, growing observably frustrated.

"Hmmmm," pondered Ossie, and he waited.

As the awkward silence built, he waited a little more. He wanted to explain himself but fought the urge.

Eventually Perry offered, "So did you deliberately turn up late this morning to see how we would handle it? To see if we would facilitate ourselves or whether we would just stand around wasting time?"

"And if I did, what could we learn from that?" asked Ossie, glad he had waited rather than explaining himself.

"Well, I guess we didn't pass the test," said Perry, looking a little embarrassed.

"The point isn't whether you pass or fail a test, Perry. The point is finding something we can learn in almost everything we do," explained Ossie. "I genuinely wanted to see if you were over-reliant on my presence in the meeting. I mean, I get that this is where you are going to raise your impediments and I can hardly do anything about them if I am not aware of them but do you actually need me here in order to update each other on how things are going and what needs to be done today?"

Don't Break The Silence

Ossie ran an experiment in order to highlight whether the team were over-reliant on him in the daily scrum and, therefore, whether they were using it for its proper purpose. He made a point with his absence, effectively asking the team, "Your ScrumMaster isn't here, how will you react?" When Ossie didn't show up on time, the team had no option but to consider this question on their own. However, it turned out that the team needed a little more prodding to come to an answer. Ossie wasn't afraid to coach the team on this topic directly.

An important aspect of "ask the team" is to give the team space and time to properly consider the question and answer it. That's why Ossie fought the urge to offer his own explanation. Different cultures have different levels of comfort with silence. In the UK it's around the 9 or 10 second mark; in Scandinavia I have learned it's a bit longer (especially first thing in the morning!) but eventually someone in the team will break the silence. This is almost always preferable to the ScrumMaster breaking the silence because it forces the team to reflect and come up with an explanation or solution of their own. It is an important part of a team's development as a self-managing unit and also reinforces the lack of authority in the ScrumMaster role.

A good ScrumMaster should never be afraid to expose the "elephant in the room." The best ScrumMasters know, though, that the collective problem solving skills of the team are much stronger, and much more conducive to team bonding, than any solution the ScrumMaster might put forth. That's why great ScrumMasters say what needs to be said, but also leave an appropriate amount of silence and space for the team to think, act, and solve on its own.

"Eventually someone in the team will break the silence."

RETRAINED

Resourceful

*"The courage to imagine the otherwise is
our greatest resource."*

Daniel J. Boorstin

I would like to clarify straight away that, when I say that ScrumMasters should be resourceful, I do not mean a ScrumMaster should be able to "do more with less" although the adage of "if life gives you lemons, then make lemonade" can be incredibly appropriate for the ScrumMaster at times. Resourceful, here, means to adopt an "art of the possible" attitude. In other words, assume a solution is possible and achieve some movement towards that solution, no matter how small or circuitous.

A ScrumMaster will be faced with many impediments, both within the team and within the wider organisation. Some may be easily resolved but many will take serious effort and time, so being resourceful—open to creative ways of moving your team and organisation forward—is a great characteristic to have.

Great ScrumMasters are proactive, pioneering and they hate monotony. They typically adopt the attitude that things are possible no matter how difficult they may appear and are constantly looking for new ways to engage their team and to inspire curiosity and energy in their team.

When considering how to solve a problem, resourceful ScrumMasters challenge *all* of their assumptions about an impediment. They will ask themselves questions such as:

- Do I really have to speak to that person about it?
- Do we even need to remove this impediment?
- If I had to explain this problem to my son/daughter/niece/nephew, how would I explain it? What would they suggest?

Many resourceful ScrumMasters broaden their perspectives and find new solutions by imagining what would make a problem *worse*, as opposed to better. Many people find taking a destructive approach to a problem not only is more natural but also is a lot easier than taking a constructive approach. Turning the problem upside down in this way can lead to insightful discoveries as to how to improve tough situations. For example, if the team are struggling with access to a particular person for information, asking "How could I make this worse?" might lead to "How would we cope if this person left the company?" If I consider this, I may find alternative strategies for coping without this person.

> **TIP** To stimulate resourcefulness, play a creativity game such as "100 uses" where you challenge yourself to think of 100 ways to use an everyday object such as a paperclip.

Resourcefulness is also very important when it comes to the application and uptake of Scrum in the wider organisation. Finding ways to encourage support for Scrum, protect fledgling teams or clear challenging organisational impediments such as resourcing or reward models can be the difference between Scrum bedding in to the organisation or dying out before it has even had a chance.

Great ScrumMasters realise that they can't do all of this on their own and so make every effort to develop their network both within the organisation and outside. Knowing how things get done within the company, how impediments get resolved and who to go and speak to about certain issues is one of the factors that separate the good ScrumMasters from the great. This, coupled with broadening your perspectives by building a network of people from outside your direct environment, will help increase your resourcefulness and the effectiveness in your role.

> **TIP** Search out ScrumMasters from other organisations – ideally those that are the most different from yours and share experiences. User groups are a good start but great ScrumMasters usually establish more focused relationships such as ScrumMaster circles. These circles are usually no larger than six people who meet up either face-to-face or virtually on a regular basis to discuss their latest challenges or thoughts. Perhaps you could even try a ScrumMaster exchange program—swap a ScrumMaster with another company for a retrospective, or even a whole sprint?

"What? What's this? Umm…"

Sex Up Your Scrum

A good ScrumMaster ensures team members share their status efficiently with one another in the daily scrum. A great ScrumMaster ensures the daily scrum is an energising event that teams look forward to.

The daily scrum is a really important part of the Scrum framework. It is the team's opportunity to check in with each other, assess their progress against their sprint commitment and collaboratively plan their day. Unfortunately a lot of teams don't seem to get the most out of these potentially crucial self-management sessions. Take the Spartans, for instance.

It was 9:05. Most of the Spartans were in their Scrum room waiting to start the daily scrum. One team member, Don, was five minutes late and the team wanted to wait until he got there before they started. Just as Harvey, the ScrumMaster, was about to give up on Don and get things going, Don rushed in, apologising profusely.

"Nightmare morning," he said. "Sue isn't well so I had to do the school run, then I got caught in the traffic coming back across town. I really needed a coffee after all that and the queue was horrendous so I had to grab one from the first floor instead. I almost wish I hadn't bothered at all, it's so bad."

"Did you come along the ring road, Don?" his teammate Peter asked.

"Yeah, why?"

"It's just that there's a much quicker route through the back roads…" Peter began.

"Umm, guys…do you think we could share travel tips after the meeting? It's just we're already behind schedule," interrupted Harvey.

"Sure. Sorry," Don apologised again.

"So who wants to kick us off this morning?" Harvey asked.

"I will," TJ offered. "Well yesterday, as you know I was re-configuring and optimising the database schema by reviewing the indexing and primary keys." TJ then showed everyone a diagram of the new index tree and began to talk the team through it. "I added a couple of non-clustered indexes here…"

As TJ continued, Harvey noticed that a few of the team didn't seem to be concentrating on what TJ was saying. In fact Peter seemed to be picking up his previous instructions to Don by drawing him a map. A couple of other team members were already looking at their watches, presumably waiting for their chance to leave.

"TJ," said Harvey. "Sorry to interrupt. That sounds like excellent stuff, but that might be a little too in-depth for the needs of this meeting. I expect there will be a couple of other people in the team who will find that index tree really useful so it would be great if we could find a nice visible place for it in the team space. Would you be available at all today for anyone if they need a bit of help understanding it?"

"Sure," TJ answered. "I've got a clear run on the index defragmentation today and you all know where I am…"

"Thanks, TJ. Who do you want to hear from next?" Harvey asked.

"Um…Peter," TJ said.

"Well, we haven't got much time left so I'll be really quick," said Peter. I was working on integrating the new feed yesterday and it turned out to be corrupted so I'll still be working on that one. If TJ could help me get the file validated that would be a big help. And I want to hear next from Don."

It was 9:30 by the time the daily scrum ended. As the team shuffled out of the room, Harvey noticed that they were mumbling and generally looking a bit miserable. He decided he needed to do something about these meetings before things got out of hand.

The next day Harvey brought in a couple of props. At dead on 9:00 Harvey shut the door and started the meeting, even though Don again wasn't there.

"I've noticed a lack of energy in these meetings recently and thought I would try and shake things up a little," Harvey began. "The aim remains the same: for everyone to get a feel for where we are as a team and what we need to focus on today, and the rest of the sprint. However, just because the meeting has a prescribed format, doesn't mean we can't change it up a little.

"The first thing we are going to do is focus on the cards rather than the people," he continued. "Rather than go round from person to person, we will go through the sprint backlog from card to card and get a feel for progress that way. It might not work but it could give us a different perspective on things.

"The next thing I want us to use is this toy bomb from one of my kids' games. It goes off at a random time. We'll pass it to whoever is speaking. Then, whoever is holding it when it goes off will have a consequence to face. But that doesn't mean you can just throw it to the next person too quickly; if the team feel they need more information from you, then you will have to take the bomb back."

A couple of the team giggled at the somewhat juvenile approach but most of them seemed keen to give it a go. One of them picked the first card from the task board and began talking, passing the bomb from person to person as they all added their input to the status of the cards. When Don came in, he was immediately thrown the bomb and asked if he wanted to add anything to the current discussion.

"What? What's this? Umm…" he looked a little confused and flustered and, just then, the bomb buzzed, surprising him even further.

The team explained their new process and his face changed from confusion to understanding.

"OK, so what's my forfeit?" he asked.

"Well I think determining future forfeits is something we need to work out as a team but, just to get things started, pick a card," Harvey said, offering a fanned-out deck of index cards.

Don picked one and read it out, "Share something embarrassing about when you were a child…Oh jeez!"

Keep It Fresh

Although the daily scrum has a prescribed format of answering three questions, it doesn't have to be a repetitive meeting that teams dread every morning. The first step for many ScrumMasters is to help teams make the most effective use of the meeting so that they get the benefit from the information sharing opportunity without the risk of it overrunning and dragging on. Much has been written about keeping people on track, managing the time, taking discussions off-line, etc. and many ScrumMasters are really good at keeping the meetings within the timebox.

However, efficiency can lead to monotony if you aren't careful. Answering the same questions with the same people at the same time every day can become a little tedious. So the best ScrumMasters have all found interesting ways to "sex up" their teams' daily scrums. The ideas that Harvey came up with in the story—moving from card to card instead of person to person, and using a toy bomb to add a bit of fun and remind people to be concise—are just two of many techniques that will liven up the daily scrum:

- Have individual countdown timers.
- Use a "bored" buzzer that anyone in the team can hit if they feel it's getting boring.
- Start the meeting with a joke, a "guess the song from the lyric", or a "guess the movie from the quote" competition.
- Begin the meeting with a trivia question and keep score throughout the sprint, or start with a fun fact about a member of the team.
- Introduce food or drink, e.g. pastries, fruit, or coffee.
- Give your update in the style of someone else (perhaps another member of the team, or a famous person). Maybe award a point for the person who can guess who you are impersonating?
- Draw your updates in a Pictionary style.

- Change the time of the daily scrum. Some teams find that having their daily scrum at the end of the day is a nice way to close out the day (especially if people all start at different times). Plus, they don't then have to remember what they did yesterday and they all know what they are picking up when they come in the next morning.
- Change the location of the daily scrum. A different space can create a different energy within the team. Some teams even have their daily scrums on the move, in a walk-and-talk style; they find the movement gives them an extra edge.
- Add an extra element to the 3 questions. For example, "something I appreciated about a member of the team yesterday," "something I am hopeful about" or "something I am worried about."
- Have a bullshit bingo [1] card with words you are not allowed to use in the daily scrum.

For more inspiration on keeping your Scrum ceremonies fresh and fun, check out Paul Goddard's card games [2].

\multicolumn{4}{c	}{Wizard Sleeves' Daily Scrum Bingo}
Cloud	Server	Management	Looking Into
Check Out	Nearly Finished	Win:Win	He/She
Same As Yesterday	Waiting for	Touch base	Environment
No Impediments	I can't remember	Ready for Test	Done My Bit

An example Bullshit Bingo card from the Wizard Sleeves team

I am sure your team could come up with something interesting and fun that would make the meeting more useful to them. Put it to them to help you come up with some ideas that will get them excited about the daily scrum again.

Act | Diverge | Account | Probe

Involve | Visualise | Expose

Be ADAPTIVE in Retrospectives

*A good ScrumMaster helps
the team identify improvements.
A great ScrumMaster inspires
the team to be ADAPTIVE.*

Retrospectives are a crucial part of the agile approach. No iteration can ever be completely perfect and no iteration can ever be an unmitigated failure. Understanding this is integral to the *inspect and adapt* process of Scrum and other agile methods. My heart sinks, therefore, when I see teams going through the motions with their retrospectives and never actually improving.

If teams are coming to multiple retrospectives with the same problems, I would consider this to be a failure of the ScrumMaster. Not because the ScrumMaster hasn't removed the impediment but because the ScrumMaster hasn't created an environment where the team can improve their situation.

Great ScrumMasters encourage their teams to be ADAPTIVE:
Act, Diverge, Account, Probe, Try, Involve, Visualise, and Expose.

Act on Improvements

Teams often come up with "we should communicate better" in their retrospectives. There's nothing wrong with that. Who can argue against improved communication? You might even see some improvements just by noting the problem. However, the default reaction of a great Scrum-Master in these situations is to ask the team to be specific. Who needs to communicate better with whom? What do they need to communicate better about? When does this communication need to happen? How will we know communication is good enough?

While there is no specific requirement for teams to leave the retrospective with an action plan where each action is assigned to someone, simply building the resulting actions into the sprint backlog of the next sprint often ensures something happens as a result of the retrospective.

While it's great to have an action plan, the team should take on a manageable number (one to three) of improvement actions each retrospective. It is much more important that the team get into the habit of small and regular improvements than to try and fix everything straight away.

Diverge Before Converging

Quite often, teams that are new to the concept of self-management and participatory decision-making will feel uncomfortable the entire time that the decision is pending. As soon as any semblance of agreement arises, the team jump on it as an opportunity to end the ambiguity and relax. This isn't always a bad thing but it is usually sub-optimal. Great ScrumMasters get the team comfortable with uncertainty and guide them through the process of divergent thinking: coming up with multiple alternatives before converging on the best solution.

One simple technique that has worked really effectively is called The Rule of Seven, as first explained to me by actor and author Lee Devin, who had witnessed it from a team at Boeing. With this technique, the team agrees that they won't make any decision until they have thought of at least seven different alternative solutions. I've found that the first few solutions or ideas are fairly easy to come up with and, usually, fairly sensible as well. Ideas four and five are typically a little more off-the-wall and take a little longer to emerge. Ideas six and, especially, seven are sometimes a bit crazy. In ideas six & seven, though, are often the seeds of ground-breaking ideas that can really energise a team and lead to quite astounding solutions.

Account for Follow Through

As we observed in the "Holding To Account" chapter, a good Scrum-Master will hold team members accountable when necessary, while a great ScrumMaster will hold teams accountable for not holding their teammates to account. This holds true in the retrospective as much as anywhere. It can be incredibly frustrating and demotivating if the same ideas, complaints or observations come up time and again. Once the team have committed to taking action, the team should ensure that they follow through on this commitment. This could be by transferring the actions on to the upcoming sprint's backlog, or simply that during the next retrospective the team go through their previous actions.

Probe for Understanding

Great ScrumMasters often take on the role of team coach, asking questions of the team to help them reflect on their situation, establish the root cause of their challenge and find a way forward. Too often, it's the other way around: the team asks the ScrumMaster questions looking for help and answers.

When you are asked a question it can take a lot of focussed effort to avoid giving an answer—it's natural, it's often what we have been trained to do and it seems rude not to. And why wouldn't you want to give an answer, especially when someone is quite plainly asking for help? Well part of the theory is that those who answer their own questions and come up with their own solutions are more empowered and more likely to succeed.

To help new ScrumMasters get used to asking meaningful and helpful questions, the ORID structure [3] offers a useful way of structuring their inquiry.

The first stage is asking *observational* or *objective* questions, such as What happened? Who said what? When did it happen? The aim here is to gather some facts about the situation without interpreting or analysing them.

The second stage is asking *reflective* questions such as How did that affect you? How do you feel about that? How do you think others were affected by that? The aim here is to learn about how the team feels about the situation.

The third stage is to ask *interpretive* questions, such as Why do you think that happened? What do you think that means? How do you think that will affect you/them/the organisation? The aim here is to understand the meaning or significance of the situation.

The fourth stage is to ask *decisional* questions, such as What are you going to do? How could you move this forward? What would you consider a positive outcome? The aim here is to help the team make some progress, or at least make a plan to make progress.

After all of these types of questions, we come to the powerful questions. A powerful question is one that causes curiosity, intrigue and often touches a deep meaning. A powerful question usually requires a paradigm shift for it to be answered. You can usually notice when you have asked a powerful question because it is usually followed by one or more of the following:

- A shift in body posture, perhaps a tilt of the head or a change in how they are sitting.
- A period of silent contemplation, which you must be very careful not to fill no matter how tempting it is.
- A noticeable change in energy.

It's quite difficult to give examples of generic, re-usable powerful questions as they are often context-specific, but here are a few that can work in many situations:

- How do you want it to be?
- What was humorous about the situation?
- What are you assuming about this situation that *might not* be true?
- If you were going to create an analogy of the situation, what would it be?
- What is surprisingly difficult for you here?
- If your life depended on taking some form of action, what would you do?

Great ScrumMasters help teams probe their own challenges. It's a little bit like teaching people to fish rather than giving them a fish.

Try Something New

Not only are retrospectives a great time to discuss, learn and come up with actions, they are also a great time to identify and/or run experiments. Of course retrospectives aren't the only time that teams should be trying things; getting a team to a place where they have the time, space and courage to experiment during the sprint is a great achievement. However, experimentation usually begins in retrospectives if it is going to begin at all. There are a number of things you can do as ScrumMaster to help here and most of them are to do with redefining what failure means.

When I was a ScrumMaster at BT, I remember one of our senior managers stating that we, as a company, were redefining what failure meant for us as a company. No longer would failure mean making the wrong decision. Now making the wrong decision was a good thing—so long as we made that decision quickly, cheaply and in good faith, we didn't make the same mistake twice, and we learned from that decision how to get better. This public statement helped tremendously when trying to encourage people to deal with the uncertainty and numerous possibilities around them.

One example of redefining failure I have seen in teams is to introduce the concept of the failure bow [4], a ceremony where a team member whose experiment led to an unsuccessful outcome literally takes a bow and accepts a round of applause for the effort. It is important to note that we are not glorifying failure here but rather changing the way we perceive and deal with it. We reward the effort, transparency and unexpected learning instead.

There is a saying that in scientific (and, in particular, iterative) experimentation, you learn the most when you have a 50 percent chance of failure because half of the possible scenarios will be eliminated. However, it can be a daunting prospect for a team to enter into something knowing that they have a 50 percent chance of an undesirable outcome. One aspect of redefining failure is to restate the value of experiments so we are not necessarily valuing the outcome but instead valuing the learning, regardless of the result. Another thing I have seen reduce anxiety here is to take a set-based approach to experimentation, running multiple simultaneous experiments to test multiple hypotheses. Almost without exception, the most successful Scrum teams I have seen have had a ScrumMaster that has created an environment where teams don't accept limiting beliefs such as "but that will never happen here." When they identify opportunities to improve, they will act first and justify later (see the upcoming "Forgiveness and Permission" chapter). If things work out as the team predict, they are lauded for their initiative or perhaps aren't even noticed. If things don't work out, then the team can explain themselves and justify why they did what they did.

The larger the organisation, the more bureaucracy is involved in making a decision. However, the larger the organisation, the greater opportunity there is for a team's action to go unnoticed or for inertia to stop something that is underway and seems to be working.

Involve Everyone

This may sound like an obvious thing for a ScrumMaster to do but it is easily overlooked in practice. It is important for a team to know that everyone is contributing but people will only contribute if they feel safe to do so. This feeling may take time to develop. A team where everyone feels able and willing to contribute to their maximum is going to be a more productive and happier team.

Visualize Data to help guide Progress

Scrum as a process and the ScrumMaster role in particular are sometimes analogised as holding a mirror up to the team, allowing them to see themselves and their behaviours in order to inspect and adapt. This mirror can be simply capturing the data from the sprint burndown and other hard data. It can also involve more soft data about what the Scrum-Master observes with regard to the team dynamics. Again, although the retrospective is an ideal time to examine data, it is valuable to have metrics such as downtime, stories completed, or impediments cleared/in progress on display continually.

One of the Scrum values is courage—ScrumMasters need this in spades as they tackle many issues with team dynamics that are easier ignored. It is often difficult to call a team to account on their (lack of) attention to quality but making data visible is one way to make sure it is always in focus. One great tactic I have seen the great ScrumMasters employ is to ask the team what they want to be held to account on, or what is important to them. This way the ScrumMaster has been granted permission to make note of progress in this area, making it much easier for them to do so. Another great tactic here is to work with the team to discover their values and create a chart, such as a radar/spider diagram, to monitor team progress on this over time. (See the "Assess Your Way To Maturity" chapter for more detail.)

Expose the Elephants

Most teams have at least one problem that they are currently ignoring, avoiding or skirting around. This is known as the elephant in the room—a big, uncomfortable topic that everyone knows should be addressed but may seem insurmountable. As with anything, if the elephant is avoided for long enough, the team will develop coping mechanisms. The problem is, these coping mechanisms don't deal with the issue and actually make the problem even less likely to be removed because it doesn't seem quite as necessary any more.

Great ScrumMasters courageously expose, and encourage teams to explore, the elephants in the room as soon as they notice them. They don't judge, but neither will they let their team tolerate and get dragged down by these problems. Instead, they offer to lead an exploration. For example, the elephant in the room could be that one of the team members is getting into the office later and later. The team are accommodating him by shifting the daily scrum and, sometimes, writing up their conversations but this is leading to inefficient teamwork and resentment is growing in the team.

Before this spirals into outright anger and rebellion, the team should confront and solve the problem.

There are two ways to look at the fact that retrospectives were included into the Scrum framework. They can either be a great, built-in opportunity for teams to improve the process every sprint or a responsibility placed upon teams as payoff for the extra autonomy and respect they are granted within Scrum. In reality it is probably healthy to take a balanced view involving both of those perspectives but, either way, retrospectives can be incredibly powerful if teams are ADAPTIVE.

*"Retrospectives... Just another opportunity
for a blame-storming session."*

The Repetitive Retrospective

A good ScrumMaster holds a balanced retrospective.
A great ScrumMaster holds a focussed retrospective

As I mentioned in the previous chapter, retrospectives are a powerful part of the Scrum framework and an essential element of the team's process of self-management and continuous improvement. However, just like the daily scrums, these meetings can be easily misunderstood, abused or lose their impact by becoming monotonous.

Kurt's team was no exception. Kurt had just been appointed ScrumMaster of the Transformers team. Their company had recently moved to Scrum and they were just finishing their first sprint. It had been an interesting, challenging and ultimately rewarding few weeks. Kurt was keen to finish the sprint off well so was preparing to facilitate the team's first sprint retrospective. At the morning's daily scrum he mentioned that he was going to be spending some time today planning tomorrow's retrospective. He was surprised to hear a few grumbles from the rest of the team. His teammate Dan even mentioned that he might be too busy to make it to the retrospective tomorrow, which disappointed Kurt.

After the daily scrum, Kurt had a quick word with Dan and asked him about his plans for the next day.

"Well to be honest," Dan said. "I'm not that keen on going anyway. I've never enjoyed those types of meetings."

"What do you mean?" Kurt asked. "This is the first one."

"Yeah, but it's just the same old thing by another name, isn't it?" Dan said. "Just another opportunity for a blame-storming session."

"Well, that's not how I understand it; and it's certainly not how I intend to run it either," replied Kurt.

Kurt explained the prime directive to Dan. He told Dan that he was following the premise set forth by Norm Kerth [5]: "Regardless of what we discover, we understand and truly believe that everyone did the best job they could, given what they knew at the time, their skills and abilities, the resources available, and the situation at hand."

Kurt then went on to explain that his plan was to lead the team to objectively look back at what happened with the sole purpose of enabling the team to work out how to make the next sprint even more successful. He assured Dan that there would be recognition of team and individual achievements during the sprint and also a non-judgemental critique of areas for potential improvement.

Dan agreed to give Kurt, and the retrospective process, a chance. He was pleasantly surprised as the team managed to highlight both the things that were going well and also the areas where they could improve without anyone being held out to dry. Perhaps this was different from the old "project post-mortems," Dan thought.

Kurt continued with this process for a couple more sprints but, after a while, he noticed that the retrospectives seemed to be becoming a little mundane and repetitive. The team didn't seem anywhere near as keen to attend as they used to. At the end of one retrospective he asked the team to do a retrospective on the retrospective, something that got a little giggle from the team before they realised he was serious.

During the retrospective's retrospective, the team indicated that they were, indeed, bored of answering the same questions every time and felt the meeting was becoming a bit too predictable and repetitive. Kurt thanked the team for the feedback and promised he would think of something different for next time. During the sprint, Kurt continued to rack his brain, and he searched the Internet looking for inspiration. He saw a number of different variations from the traditional format, discovering some new questions to ask as well. He found a number of ideas for techniques he could use within the retrospective by reading *Agile Retrospectives* [6] by Esther Derby and Diana Larsen. Still, nothing felt exactly right for the next retrospective.

The answer came when he was talking to the product owner about what the goal for the next sprint might be. It occurred to Kurt that the team had really taken to the concept of sprint goals (see Chapter "Sprint Goals") so he thought that perhaps it might be worth experimenting with the idea of a retrospective goal. During the next retrospective, Kurt asked the team to imagine that, instead of being at this retrospective, they were just about to start the sprint review meeting of the upcoming sprint—to imagine that they were in the future and looking back on the really successful sprint they had just finished. Once everyone indicated that they had a mental image of this situation, he asked them to describe the moral of the sprint: a maxim that explained why they were a healthier, more productive, better team than they were a sprint ago. To help them get started Kurt gave a couple of examples:

"Don't talk to strangers" might reflect that we stopped getting distracted from our sprint goal.

"Look both ways before you cross" might reflect that we finally solved our quality issues by instigating tighter peer review and QA controls within the team.

Once everyone had a moment to think, they were asked to complete the sentence "And the moral of the sprint is…" on an index card and hand it in. When all the cards were complete, the team clustered the cards and identified a common theme, which was around the truth that having one completed story was more valuable than two partially completed stories. The moral? A bird in the hand is worth two in the bush.

"We now have a goal for this retrospective," claimed Kurt. "Let's spend the rest of the retrospective working out what we need to do to make this goal a reality."

The Hook [7]

In all my time as a ScrumMaster, coach and consultant, I've not heard of any sprint that has been an unmitigated success. Nor have I heard of any sprint that has been an unmitigated disaster either. A celebration may make the team feel good but it won't necessarily help them improve. Equally ineffective is listing all the things that went wrong. It may be thorough but it certainly won't lead to a motivated, engaged team who are hungry to improve. Therefore, it is imperative that a ScrumMaster holds a balanced retrospective.

95% of ScrumMasters hold balanced retrospectives as if they were second nature. However, not that many hold focussed retrospectives. Hollywood screenwriters talk about the first ten pages of the film script having to contain "a hook," something that intrigues the reader/audience and pulls them in. The best movies all have a hook. Think of the iconic scenes from *The Godfather*, *The Shining*, *Up*, *Jaws* or *The King's Speech* and you can imagine what I mean by "the hook." All the great ScrumMasters I have seen ensure their retrospectives have a hook as well—something that sets the scene for what is about to happen while also pulling people in, grabbing their interest and energising them.

There are a few common ways of coming up with a retrospective goal:

At The Start Of The Retrospective

Ask the team to help you craft a goal during the first couple of minutes:

- Ask every member of the team to describe the sprint in a word or two, or perhaps as an abstract object such as "if the sprint were a chocolate bar, what would it be?" Then cluster the outputs and find a theme before focussing the sprint on that theme.

- Use a game like Remember The Future [8], which is similar to the "moral of the sprint" exercise in the story.

- Ask the team (or perhaps small groups within the team) to come up with a sprint limerick or song that defines either the past sprint or the one that is about to happen. Use that output as something to either aim for or to investigate.

During The Sprint

Somewhere in the team space, set up a number of boxes or envelopes where team members can post their thoughts as they come up. These boxes could be labelled anything, from "frustrations" or "ideas" to "appreciations" or perhaps "achievements." In the sprint retrospective, empty the boxes and ask the team to craft a goal from the accumulated notes.

Follow Your Nose

There is always room for good old ScrumMaster intuition. During the sprint, ScrumMasters are in a privileged position, able to see a lot of what is going on with a certain detachment. They can, and should, be listening to what is being said and what is not being said, looking out for good examples of team dynamics and development as well as opportunities for further team growth. Great ScrumMasters have no issue with starting the retrospective with a challenge based on their own observations, for example, "This sprint I have noticed a larger proportion of time than normal has been spent on fixing defects. I wonder if it would be a good idea to take some time out to explore why this might be and what we could do about it."

"All the great ScrumMasters I have seen ensure their retrospectives have a hook"

A

RETRAINED

Alternative

*"Make your own kind of music,
sing your own special song."*

Mama Cass

Working as a servant-leader is an alternative approach for many people and organisations. Servant-leaders flatten the hierarchies of their organisations, tear up old standards and challenge the traditions and institutionalised working processes of their companies. At some point, all ScrumMasters will be faced with the prospect of introducing some radical concepts to the team and the organisation in order to continue the journey to a more responsive, high-performing agile structure.

Great ScrumMasters are prepared to stand out and break the mould. They pioneer new techniques and strategies in the pursuit of excellence and performance no matter how counter-culture they may seem. Even after many years of experimenting with Scrum, the path is still not well trodden and there is still no blueprint for how organisations should be structured and organised in order to be successful. Therefore ScrumMasters must be prepared to challenge the status quo and do things differently.

This doesn't mean that ScrumMasters should be contrary merely for the sake of it. It does, however, often mean that great ScrumMasters will have to go against the grain of conventional wisdom and, almost certainly, take the more difficult option available to them if the easier option is likely to not be radical enough to alter long-term behaviour.

As teams develop and grow, there will even be opportunities to look for alternatives to some of the Scrum practices, especially when the team reach Ri. Be prepared to stand up and stick your head up above the crowd but, when you do, be on the lookout for anything that might be coming to try to cut you down to size. Always remember Schwaber's advice that a dead ScrumMaster is a useless one; pick your battles and find ways to push for change in a tactful way.

TIP Seek out alternative perspectives from different industries or paradigms. For example observe how teachers manage a classroom. Also take time out to seek out innovative and inspiring ideas (TED.com is a great place to start) and see how these ideas may apply to your situation. Another idea is to play an abstract game such as "The Marshmallow Challenge" [1] or "The Penny Game" [2] with a group to see what parallels the team can draw from something fun to their real situation.

*Teams with more T-shaped people
are not only more resilient and responsive
but are also more collaborative and creative.*

T-Shaped People

*A good ScrumMaster
encourages teams to share skills.
A great ScrumMaster encourages
teams to share responsibilities.*

In the early stages of adopting Scrum at your organisation, creating a cross-functional team is often a big challenge. If the team isn't cross-functional, then they will find it nearly impossible to get anything done (as in potentially shippable) in a sprint. That's why staffing the team with the appropriate mix of skills has to be one of the ScrumMaster's primary objectives. Most new Scrum teams are made of I-shaped people—people who have a depth of skill in one particular area, like coding or testing or user interface design, but not much skill in areas outside their speciality. Their skills, therefore, are deeper than they are broad, resembling the sans-serif letter I.

Design   Analysis   Develop   Test   Architect

An example of an I-shaped person

This I shape is particularly appropriate because it also reflects the typical mindset: This is what I do, who I am and I am very good at this particular skill. It defines me. Being I-shaped has advantages: a depth of knowledge makes a person highly efficient at accomplishing work in that area. At the same time, though, it introduces a great deal of risk, because each team might have only one person who can accomplish a particular task. As my friend Aislinn Green used to say, I-shaped people have a high "lotto factor", describing the risk to the team if that person wins the lotto and doesn't come back to work.

That's why great ScrumMasters encourage people to develop cross-functional, T-shaped, skill-sets. "T-shaped people" were touted as the engine of creativity and success at IDEO by their CEO, Tim Brown. [3] T-shaped people are so named because the vertical shaft of the T represents the depth of their chosen or preferred skill, while the horizontal bar of the T represents the diversity of other skills they can dip into in order to collaborate.

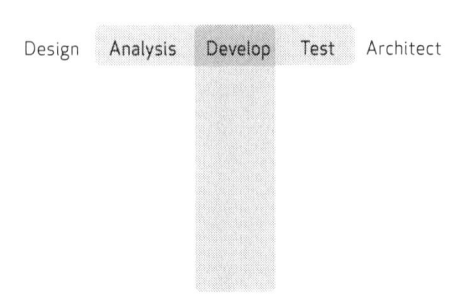

An example of a T-shaped person

Teams with more T-shaped people are not only more resilient and responsive but are also more collaborative and creative. Teams with T-shaped people also don't have to worry about the risk associated with having only one person with a particular skill.

T-shaped doesn't just have to refer to skills though. Scrum teams are expected to do whatever is required of them to deliver within a sprint. This often means people need to act outside of their job description and take responsibility for tasks that they are not technically responsible for, or necessarily highly skilled at. The Geckos are a good example of a team that needed a more T-shaped mindset.

The Geckos were coming towards the end of the sprint (day 28 of 30) and were holding their daily scrum. The team were standing around the sprint backlog board and were taking it in turns to update the rest of the team on what they had been working on and their plan for the day. An extract from the conversation follows:

"Guy & I have finished coding the photo upload feature and have handed it over to Roxie and Eve to test," Christian said. "We're now done for this sprint so we are probably going to make a start on the ratings feature from the product backlog to give ourselves a bit of a headstart for the next sprint. Obviously we have no impediments because we're finished! Hooray!"

Christian then threw the speaker's ball to Roxie to indicate that he wished to hear from her next, so Roxie took her turn:

"It's probably going to take us the last two days of the sprint to test. We were hoping for a handoff yesterday, but we ended up kind of hanging around a little yesterday waiting for Christian and Guy to finish. Now we have the feature ready for testing, we can get cracking on it. I am a bit worried about it as I suspect it might be a can of worms but at the moment we have no impediments."

The team then updated their very healthy-looking sprint burndown to reflect the fact that some tasks were finished a bit early. In fact, with Christian & Guy starting on some of the stuff coming up in the next

147

sprint, the team remarked that they were actually in an even healthier position than the sprint burndown implied.

It came as a bit of a surprise to the product owner Ericka, then, when she was told at the end of the sprint that the photo upload feature was not actually ready to deploy—it didn't pass testing. The sprint burndown had made it appear that the team was so far ahead that a few members had even started working on bonus features that hadn't been planned into this sprint. Yet the reality was that one of the product owner's most important features didn't get done.

In the retrospective, the team discussed what happened to cause the team to miss their commitment.

"Well we managed to get everything done our end," said Christian. "It was just the testers who didn't manage to do their stuff."

"Well, if you had managed to get it to us more quickly, we might have had a chance," Roxie replied. "We only had two days to test it. I did mention that the photo upload was likely to be a can of worms, by the way."

Marcelle, the ScrumMaster, quickly tried to defuse the situation: "Whose fault it was doesn't interest me, and I am pretty sure it doesn't interest Ericka."

Marcelle, realising the team needed to face a harsh reality stated, "What I see here is that we failed to deliver her priority #4 feature this sprint but somehow managed to find time to work on her priority #9 feature. Am I right?"

There were a couple of seconds of silence as the team processed this before Guy said, "Yes, but what were we supposed to do? Test our own work or sit around doing nothing? We had finished the coding of the photo upload feature so we moved on to the next item."

Marcelle simply responded with a question:

"What makes you believe that the testing of that feature was purely the responsibility of Roxie & Eve?"

"The fact that they are testers," they quickly answered, in unison.

If You Can't Get Done, Go Surfing

The concept of "done" is critical to Scrum. Teams do not have the luxury of being able to just do the coding this sprint and test it next sprint. In Scrum, every feature that the team takes on needs to be potentially releasable at the end of the sprint.

The "developers don't test" syndrome is probably one of the most common role clashes in Scrum teams. Because most organisations are set up around a typical waterfall lifecycle, which encourages I-shaped people, this mindset is incredibly commonplace. In Scrum, the role of developer is intended to mean a member of a self-managing team whose primary responsibility is to help the team turn product backlog items from requirements or user needs in to working functionality.

> "It is better for the developers to be surfing than writing code that won't be needed. [...] If they went surfing, they would have fun and I would have a less expensive system and fewer headaches to maintain"
> Jeff Sutherland [4]

There is no point in any member of the team getting all of their tasks complete if the features are not "done." On a software team, that's going to involve testing. If there is a bottleneck in skills, the team have a responsibility to do what needs to be done, to the best of their collective ability. And sometimes doing nothing (not adding code that can't be tested) is the best response. Rather than go off and begin writing new code, Christian and Guy should have found a way to accelerate the testing of their feature. Better yet, they should have found ways to minimize the size of their handoff to the testers in the first place by involving the testers earlier and finding ways to test something.

People whose primary skill-set is testing must be part of most Scrum teams. This does not, however, excuse the other developers from testing or allow them to abdicate responsibility for getting a feature done to the testers. Testing, and indeed quality, is a whole-team responsibility in Scrum.

Blurring The Lines

Funnily enough it is not just the developers who are concerned or anxious about blurring this boundary between development and test. There are status concerns, quality concerns, job security concerns, career progression concerns. I have seen many organisations that attach lower status to testers than they do to developers; only when you have become "good enough" are you allowed to become a developer. This rather absurd practice is nevertheless a cultural reality (re-enforced by pay rates) that some ScrumMasters may need to counter (with the help of management, HR, and so on).

Similarly, I have met many who believe that you have to have a special mindset to be a good tester. Developers, they say, are a different breed. As such, they can't be trusted to test. Again, this nonsensical point of view is almost certainly going to become self-fulfilling. The more that developers are not trusted to test, the more they will be unable to test and the more they will shirk the responsibility of writing good code.

Will spreading my skills away from pure development into the testing arena reduce my marketability? Will I have to sacrifice my focus on being the best in my field in order to learn (and implement) new skills? Am I going to have to become a hybrid? Will I miss out on some sexy new languages or coding techniques just to do more testing? These are just some of the concerns over job security and career progression that people have when facing this situation. In contrast, the growing evidence suggests (unsurprisingly) that the rates for developers with good testing/quality skills are much higher than those without.

Esther Derby says that the only way to deal effectively with turnover on teams is for each member to be doing one thing, learning another, and be teaching a third. [5] This is also the way to encourage the development of T-shaped people within Scrum teams.

Pairing developers with testers can allow testing to be undertaken during coding, and allows that code to evolve in response to the feedback of the ongoing testing process. It is much more collaborative and agile at heart than pairing developers to feed testers.

Another option is for the team to implement some form of Kanban-type limits on the stages within a sprint. For example, the team would set a limit of a maximum of two items to be "in test" at any one time. Once that limit is reached, the team then "swarm" around the items at the bottleneck stage to clear the blockage.

One team came up with a "team initiation knowledge test" that every member of the team needed to take in order to show that they could complete tasks in each discipline within the team, including test automation, database scripts, controller tests, and so on. This was eventually rolled out to potential new recruits as part of the assessment process. This same team also had sheriff and deputy badges for each discipline, with the

Alternative

sheriff's badge being worn by the lead in that area and the deputy being the person who was committed to learning that skill as backup.

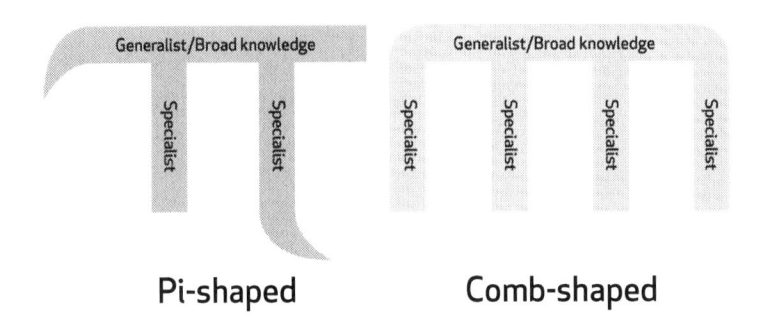

Pi-shaped   **Comb-shaped**

There are now many different shapes that people can be encouraged to grow into, but the important point is looking at how we as individuals develop our skill-sets to help the team and organisation become and stay responsive to the demands of the work and resilient to changes in demand and customer needs.

One of my favourite activities in this area is 'Competency Mapping' [6]. By mapping out the entire workflow and looking back at the definition of done and product backlog, the team can identify all of the skills and competencies needed to be able to deliver value as a team.

The team can then draw up a matrix and everyone can rate themselves in terms of their competence level for each of the skills needed to complete the work. By then asking others to rate them on their skill levels they can discuss any wild differences before agreeing an overall competency level. A competency matrix can look like this:

T-Shaped People

COMPETENCY	🔧 Tools	💭 Process	🙆 People	📝 Docs	📈 Growth
ROO	◕	◔	●	●	◐
SHANNIE	◐	●	◔	◕	◔
SHEILA	◔	◔	◕	○	◐
DEEPAK	○	◕	●	◐	◕
ASHTON	◔	◔	◔	●	◔
NIC	○	◐	◕	◐	◐
MOISES	◕	◔	◐	○	●
CALLUM	◐	○	●	◐	○
HARRIET	●	◕	◔	◔	○
SURAI	○	◕	◐	◐	◕
CAM	◔	◔	●	◕	◔
ALEX	○	●	◔	◐	●
MACKENZIE	◕	○	○	◕	◐
PRANAV	◐	◔	◕	◔	○
REMY	◔	◐	◐	◕	●
HAZEL	○	◐	◔	◐	◕
KANTU	◔	●	◕	○	◔
CHRIS	●	◔	○	◕	◐

● VERY EXPERIENCED; CAN MENTOR OTHERS
◕ SELF-SUFFICIENT
◐ SOME PRACTICAL EXPERIENCE
◔ KNOW THE THEORY BUT LITTLE PRACTICE
○ NO KNOWLEDGE OR EXPERIENCE

Alternative

However the team decide to develop their T-shaped skills, they need to understand how taking on new tasks and learning new skills will affect their current jobs, potential incentives, and future promotions. As such, ScrumMasters would do well to facilitate discussions in a clear and gentle, yet firm, manner (and possibly include an HR presence). Bear in mind that this area is definitely outside of most teams' comfort zones—but sometimes teams need to be pushed outside of their comfort zone in order to develop.

"It is better for the developers to be surfing than writing code that won't be needed."

"Is there no way that we can be a bit more pro-active here?"

Getting Stuff "Done"

*A good ScrumMaster helps a team meet
their definition of done at the end of the sprint.
A great ScrumMaster helps a team extend
their definition of done.*

Scrum calls for a cross-functional team to commit to getting an increment of the product to a state of "potentially releasable" every sprint. To do this, we must arrange the work so that tasks that were previously done in a silo and then handed off are worked on in tandem or with a great deal of coordination. Plus we must learn to work closely with groups that we might not previously have interacted with much. These are tough skills to learn, as we will see in the following story of the Doomsday Bunnies. Reaching the high bar of *done* is so difficult that many Scrum teams may begin with a less stringent definition of done at first, as they learn to work in new ways. Great ScrumMasters understand the need to be practical, but quickly move the team forward to new ways of working so that they can create potentially releasable increments each and every sprint.

The Doomsday Bunnies were a newly formed cross-functional team of 10, pulled together around a new project to establish a system for monitoring, grouping and reporting of internal and external financial transactions. Rafael, the product owner, explained to the team how this system would provide cost savings of $6M, as well as offer the opportunity to increase revenues by $10M in the first six months. The team was excited about being on a new project but a little anxious about using Scrum for the first time.

Stevie, the ScrumMaster, had explained to the team that being *done* each sprint meant that everything that was coded needed to be tested as well. The team was comprised of developers Lucas, Javier, Maxine, Glen and Dirk, testers Jamie, Martin and Andrea, plus Fernando as the architect/designer and Danielle as the user experience lead.

The first sprint didn't go well. Tester Jamie and developer Glen had a big confrontation about the quality of Glen's code or Jamie's pernickety approach to testing, depending on your point of view! There also seemed to be a big mismatch in terms of who was busy at various points in the sprint. The developers seemed to be very busy at the start while the testers were under-utilised. The reverse happened towards the end of the sprint, with the testers working overtime while the developers waited for a bug to fix. Though the team had committed to eight product backlog items, they only truly completed three.

At the retrospective, the team agreed that the entire sprint felt chaotic. The developers complained that they could have gotten more coding done, but were distracted by the bug fixes they had to do instead of working on new items. The testers complained that they seemed to be the only ones concerned about quality. The team looked to Stevie expectantly, waiting for him to help them solve the problem.

Stevie described what he had observed during the sprint—two teams working in tandem, but not as one. When he asked the team for some suggestions to create a sense of unity, the team suggested that they might be better off splitting into two teams for the next sprint – the developers in one team and the testers in the other. The testers could finish testing the incomplete items from this sprint while the developers began working on new features. This would give the developers a one-sprint headstart, so that the testers would always be one sprint behind, testing what the developers had built the sprint before while the developers move on to developing the next items.

"Is an item truly done in a sprint if it's not tested?" Stevie asked.

The team reluctantly admitted that it was not. But they were stuck as to how to achieve a state of done without causing conflict and chaos.

"What if we stop thinking of testing as an activity to find defects and more of an activity to prevent defects?" Stevie asked. "Could we find ways to work as one team to get more things to a potentially shippable state inside one sprint?"

"What do you mean? Test before we code? But there's nothing to test!" replied Lucas.

"Is there no way that we can be a bit more pro-active here?" challenged Stevie.

"Well we could turn the acceptance criteria for the first couple of product backlog items into test scripts during sprint planning," said Andrea. "Then, while the developers are writing code to make those tests pass, we could be doing the same for the next couple of features."

Martin then joined in, "Where I used to work we buddied a developer with a tester and they worked together on a feature until it was developed and tested. That might work, although we would probably need another tester"

"Well, shall we try the option that is available to us to see how it goes?" asked Stevie. The team agreed to give it a try.

Alternative

Scrummerfall

Almost all new teams struggle to avoid the trap of mini-waterfalls or scrummerfalls—squeezing a traditional software development lifecycle into short iterations. This can happen inside the sprint (as happened to the team in our story) and often progresses to the testing team moving out of the sprint (as the team suggested). The end result is that the development time extends from one sprint to at least two because each item takes at least two sprints to complete, sometimes three or more.

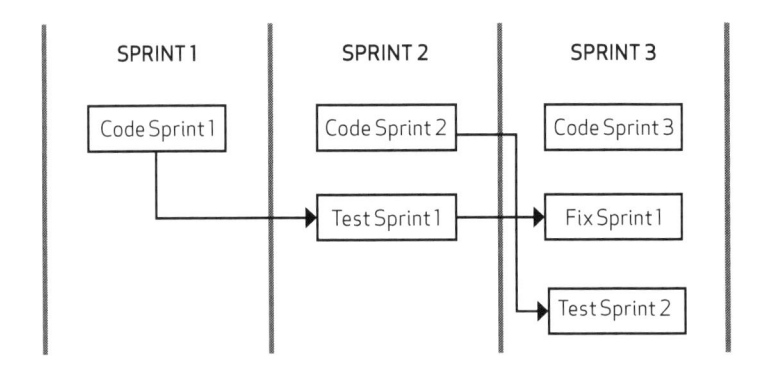

```
SPRINT 1            SPRINT 2            SPRINT 3

Code Sprint 1       Code Sprint 2       Code Sprint 3

                    Test Sprint 1       Fix Sprint 1

                                        Test Sprint 2
```

Great ScrumMasters avoid scrummerfalls and get stuff done inside a sprint by encouraging teams to find ways to integrate testing and development (and other tasks). The idea of buddying up that Martin put forward is often a healthy one in that it explicitly shifts the idea of one group or individual being responsible for the quality of the product. Quality should be a whole team responsibility not an after-thought or QA's job. This is a cultural change that will take time to embed and teams will need to be guided through it.

Engineering practices such as TDD [7] or test-first are not explicitly called out in Scrum—Scrum is completely non-committal about such things—but in common practice, most if not all of the successful Scrum teams I have come across in the IT sphere make extensive use of such practices. ScrumMasters should encourage teams to experiment with these. A note of caution here though is that despite being proven to provide massive benefits, in order to really grasp these techniques, teams need to put a lot of effort in and there is a steep learning curve.

Slow Down To Speed Up

Scrum teams, especially new ones, often need to slow down to speed up. As counter-intuitive as it might seem, taking fewer items into the sprint when a team is new and learning allows the team to find ways to work together to get those items done. Plus, partially completed work is of no value to a product owner.

Members of a Scrum team should also be aware that they do not need to be busy 100% of the time—in fact, this can lead to sub-optimal results [8]. The most effective Scrum teams acknowledge that, in order for the team to be successful, each individual needs to have some spare capacity. If the spare capacity for any individual is too high, the team should address this in the retrospective. Is there a need for a full-time member with this skill-set? Is there anything else this individual could be contributing to the team? How could the team better organise themselves to be more productive? Remember the goal is not for each *individual* to be as productive as possible but rather for the *team* to be as productive as possible. The former does not necessarily lead to the latter and, in many cases, individual optimisation leads to a diminishing of team productivity.

Done or Done Done?

I was working at one organisation that had decided to adopt Scrum because, in their words, "Things couldn't get any worse so what the heck?" Not a great reason for choosing Scrum but that's another story! Towards the end of the first sprint the team were really excited about the upcoming sprint review because they had made such great progress on their commitments.

The product owner was delighted with the demonstration; after not receiving anything of value from the team in nearly a year, getting a few features in a month was close to a miracle in her eyes. She was praising the team, praising Scrum and praising me profusely about this turnaround.

"When my users get hold of these features on Monday they are going to be so happy!" she exclaimed, at which point the developers looked at each other, a little sheepishly.

When I asked the ScrumMaster what was going on, he admitted, "When we said we were done, we didn't mean that we were done done. This stuff works on our machines but there's nothing really behind the scenes and it hasn't been tested or integrated yet. It will be another couple of months before you could actually release it."

The team had done the best they could and managed to get some functionality to a demonstrable state but it was, in the eyes of the product owner, just smoke and mirrors. Reflecting on this, the product owner admitted that although this was a much better position than she was in one month ago—she now had something she could give tangible feedback on—she was disappointed. The team realised that it would have been better to try to get one feature completely done than to have many features partially done.

Getting things done is ultimately at the heart of Scrum. The definition of what is classified as done is key. Scrum states that a feature needs to be potentially releasable by the end of the sprint for it to be considered done. This high bar means that our product owner is continually getting value delivered and our teams are getting tangible feedback on the whole of the development lifecycle every sprint. It also avoids the risk of months and months of development of features that end up being misunderstood, incorrect or faulty when we eventually get to the testing and integration phases.

Getting done in a sprint is often a huge challenge for teams and organisations in general. It usually involves gathering specialist skill-sets from around the company and forming a cross-functional team from them. It also involves changing working practices and some very ruthless and creative product backlog grooming to ensure valuable slices of functionality are being fed into the sprints.

Sometimes, teams find it impossible or impractical to meet the potentially releasable definition of done that Scrum sets. A good ScrumMaster will help the team craft a definition of done that is as good as possible at that moment in time. ScrumMasters will typically find a lot of their time in the early stages of Scrum adoption will be taken up with helping their team find ways to meet that definition of done, even if it is a watered-down version of what Scrum has asked for. While many purists will tell you this is not a good thing, we find the best solution possible to the problem that we can in our current circumstances.

Great ScrumMasters, while being practical and pragmatic, will not let the team stay too long in a less-than-optimal definition of done. Instead, they will set a target of helping the team extend their definition of done as much as possible, as quickly as possible. This almost always has the biggest impact on productivity, quality, morale and, in effect, agility. It might involve lobbying for greater training or for the transfer of an individual into a Scrum team or perhaps an investment in automation—whatever is needed to help the team get "done" in this and every subsequent sprint. Until we can do this, the best we can hope for is scrummerfall.

A little nervously Ricardo said, "Ooookaaay…sure."

Review
The Sprint Review

A good ScrumMaster facilitates the sprint review to look back and review the product built in the previous sprint. A great ScrumMaster facilitates the sprint review to look forward and shape the product in future sprints.

The sprint review is perhaps the most neglected meeting in Scrum. It is often simply labelled as a sprint demo or a show and tell, which is an important element of the meeting but certainly not its sole purpose. The sprint review shouldn't be a celebration or a narrative report; it shouldn't need any slide-based presentations or dashboard reports. It should be very tangible, interactive and practical. And there should be a discussion about what the sprint results mean for the team and the project—this is the primary opportunity for the product owner and, more importantly, the stakeholders to guide the future direction of the product.

The following story, of the Trigger Happy Bunnies team actually tells of a somewhat unconventional sprint review.

At the end of one daily scrum toward the end of the sprint, the team's product owner, Diego, popped his head in the door. "You wanted to see me, Isa?" Diego asked.

"Yep. I have an idea to run by you. I'll be right there." After the meeting finished, the two of them wandered off and, when Isa returned about twenty minutes later, the team were curious.

"What was that all about?" asked Ricardo.

"Ah, nothing much. We were just going over details of the sprint review. Just double checking the timings, location and such like," responded Isa. "By the way, there are probably going to be a few more people there than normal as the last couple of releases have gathered a bit of attention."

Ricardo wasn't convinced that he was getting the whole story from Isa but shrugged and thought little more of it.

The next day, as everyone gathered in the showcase room for the sprint review, Ricardo noticed that indeed there were a lot more people than they have had previously to such meetings. He took note of the new participants, many of whom he had never seen before and didn't know, and also the addition of donuts, fruit and drinks.

Ricardo logged in and connected the display up to their environment so that the developers could demonstrate the features they had completed this sprint. Once Ricardo was logged in, Diego stood up and made an announcement:

"I know this is a break from protocol but, this time, Isa has asked if we could do things a little differently. Rather than have the developers give the demonstration, I would like to do that part." He looked at Ricardo and added, "If that's OK, of course."

Ricardo looked around and the saw the team looking at each other. They looked a little confused and, perhaps, a little worried as well. He then looked at Isa who smiled, nodded and gave him a look that said, "It's OK. Go with it."

A little nervously Ricardo said, "Ooookaaay…sure."

Diego proceeded to run through the new features, demonstrating both the way the features worked and that he was familiar enough with them to be able to use them. Because he was experienced with how the product was to be used rather than just how it was built, he ran through the functionality in a different way than the developers would have normally.

Rory, one of the account managers whose team uses the product, asked:

"Why do we need to go through that step? It seems unnecessary and slows down the valuation process."

Diego explained the reason was because of another feature that was to be demonstrated next but, while explaining this to Rory, he realised that the features were impacting one another and needed to be separated. The team discussed the situation briefly, decided that a change was required, and added a new user story to the product backlog.

After the sprint review had finished, Isa explained to the team that he thought it made a nice change for Diego to do the demonstration part of the sprint review. He knew that because Diego had been so involved during the sprint, he knew the features and how they worked. Therefore, not only was he comfortable with what the team had been working on but he could also relate the features to the stakeholders in a different and more direct way. He also explained how it had changed the focus of the conversation a little to focus more on what could be done next.

The developers agreed that it had been helpful and also commented that it had been quite nice to sit back and listen to the product owner effectively say to the stakeholders "Look what my team have done this sprint – aren't they great?"

This one change had been a huge morale-booster for the developers. Isa believed that it would have the added benefit of further strengthening the relationship between the team and the product owner as well.

No Surprises

This product owner–led sprint review, though a bit unconventional, turned out to be one of the best sprint review meetings I have ever seen. Perhaps ironically, it actually broke one of the rules of Scrum. The sprint review is, among other things, an opportunity for the developers to demonstrate their deliveries. It is an opportunity for the product owner and stakeholders to see progress, guide the direction of the product through the use of empirical feedback and potentially realise value incrementally. It is also a chance for the developers to get feedback from the product owner (and other stakeholders) and to gain a sense of momentum from making tangible progress through the product backlog and seeing the product come together.

The sprint review is effectively a safety net built into Scrum. Before the product is public, the product owner has a chance to review what the developers have delivered. In the worst-case scenario the product owner turns up to the sprint review and tells the team they got it wrong and delivered nothing of value this sprint. It's disappointing, but the fact that these reviews happen every sprint means that any waste is minimal, especially when compared to the end-of-project release typical of waterfall development methodologies.

The more effective Scrum teams involve the product owner continually throughout the sprint, getting feedback on features in real time so that, at the sprint review, the product owner is not surprised about what has or hasn't been done and the team are not surprised by features getting rejected at the last minute. The more the product owner is involved during the sprint, the less time the team need to spend demonstrating functionality. If there are no surprises, it frees up time during the sprint review for the product owner, stakeholders, and team to proactively collaborate on the future direction of the product itself.

Try this at one of your sprint reviews, even if only the team and the product owner are in attendance; you might be surprised at how powerful (or telling) it is.

End Of Sprint Questions

To help make sprint reviews even more valuable, I encourage teams to address a number of questions in addition to demonstrating the features that have been delivered, as shown in the illustration below.

End of Sprint Questions

New Requirements?

Have we identified any new functionality that we now need? Sometimes new requirements emerge during the sprint or seeing what is now possible sparks an idea in someone about what could be done next.

New Priorities?

Have the priorities changed? For example, has the reporting feature suddenly dropped down in importance while the security feature is now more critical? Sprint reviews are a great opportunity to shift priorities around to suit the current state of the project. Perhaps one item from the product backlog is now no longer required at all, in which case it could be removed from the product backlog altogether

New Estimates?

Have our estimates changed? The sprint review is a time for the developers to revisit their estimates against some empirical data to give a more accurate view of the team's velocity. Equally important is the chance to change the estimate of something the team have yet to start because of the new information gathered during this sprint.

New Velocity?

Has our velocity changed? The team now have another data point about how much work they are capable of completing within a sprint. By revisiting their velocity projection, they should be able to increase their certainty about the likely end date or the likely scope.

New Design?

Does the design need to change? Scrum teams embrace the concept of emergent design and, as such, should revisit the design of the product at least at the end of every sprint to ensure that it remains sensible, with integrity and that they build in the appropriate amount of refactoring.

New Release?

Can we release? Ideally Scrum teams should be in a position where they could release the increment at the end of every sprint if they so decide. This might not always be the case (see the "Getting Stuff Done" chapter) and so we may use this information to guide our release and/or marketing strategy.

New Process?

Should we change our process? Most of this will be covered in the subsequent sprint retrospective but there may be some elements of this that it would be appropriate to discuss with the wider audience present for the sprint review. For example, access to UAT, team composition, feature acceptance criteria and so on.

All of these questions contribute to the overall aim of updating the plan to reflect the information that the team have now. Ultimately, the team, product owner and stakeholders must decide if this is a project that they wish to continue investing in, which is a much more valuable output from the sprint review than a mere demonstration of functionality.

RETRAINED

Inspiring

*"Do not follow where the path may lead.
Go instead where there is no path and leave a trail."*

Ralph Waldo Emerson

I see ScrumMasters as radical change agents within organisations and people who inspire energy for change in others around them. They act as catalysts, incendiary fire-starters who create a place where people want to be and are able to be their best.

Nobody is ever inspired by a cynic. Great ScrumMasters are infectiously positive and optimistic, embodying the *art of the possible* and role-modelling the values and principles of greatness. They are courageous in their convictions and ruthless in their belief in the capacity and the potential of their team and the organisation. This positivity is part of what makes great ScrumMasters such motivating people.

Great ScrumMasters will also find out what motivates the people they are serving. I was once asked in a workshop about what reward policies Scrum has built into it. When I responded with "there are none," they then asked me what they should do about it. I posed them a hypothetical scenario:

Suppose, at the end of the project, your boss comes along and says "Great job! That was a really impressive piece of work and it meant a lot to me and the rest of the company. I would like to recognise your effort and performance but I don't know how. How can I reward you? Name it…"

I asked the group to think about it and then asked them what they would ask for. The responses I got included:

- "It would just be nice if someone actually said something like that!"
- Money
- Time off
- New gadgets
- Company-sponsored social events
- Time and authority to improve the team's work environment
- More autonomy over the team's work
- An opportunity to experiment with new tools or technologies

And then one lady said:

"It's funny you should ask because just recently I got something that I didn't know I wanted but, now that I've had it, I want it all the time."

The rest of the group looked at her and fell expectantly silent, as if to say, "What is this magical thing of which you speak?!"

She explained that, at the last sprint review, the ScrumMaster had arranged with the product owner to bring along a couple of the actual end users of the product to see the latest features that had been developed and to give a little feedback on the previous release. It turned out that the developers had heard rumours about end users but had never met one and hadn't before had the opportunity to speak to them. Hearing directly that what they had been working on day in and day out was not only actually being used but also that it was having a positive impact on people's working lives was a massively motivating factor.

The rest of the group nodded in agreement. We then discussed how this opportunity is actually built into Scrum with the sprint review.

> **TIP** Find out what motivates the individuals within your team and what motivates them collectively as a team. These are unlikely to be the same thing. You may also be surprised by what you find out and how simple it may be to meet those needs.

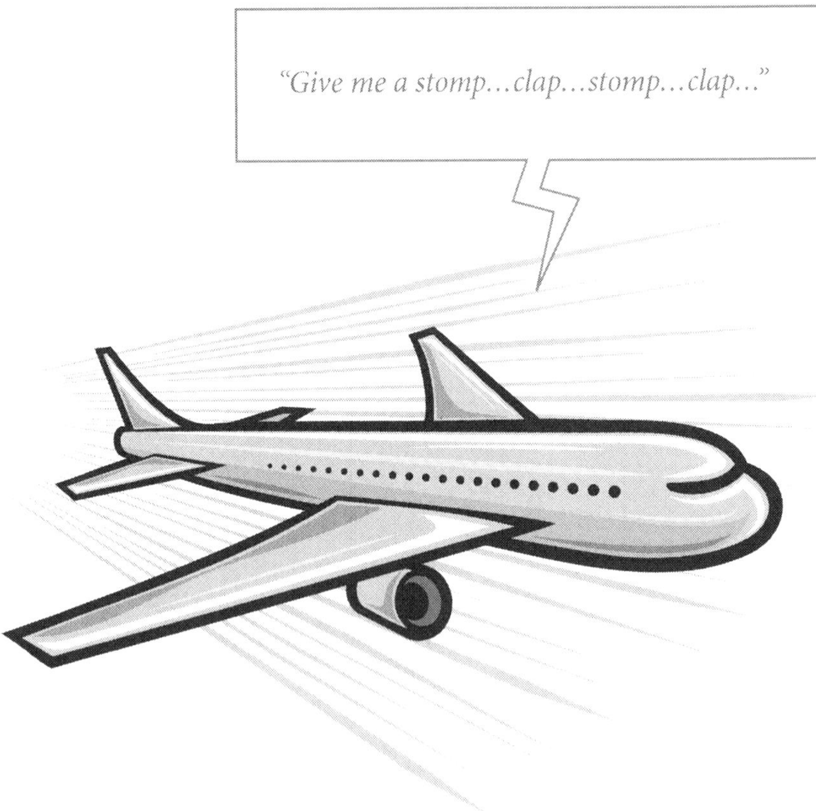
"Give me a stomp…clap…stomp…clap…"

Invoking Creativity

*A good ScrumMaster creates an
environment where raising impediments can occur.
A great ScrumMaster creates an environment
where creativity can occur.*

A ScrumMaster's first job is often getting teams to a point where they can share status and raise impediments freely (see "A Tale Of Two Scrums"). While this isn't too much of a challenge for most good ScrumMasters, the ScrumMasters that set themselves apart are those that can take the team to a point where they actually begin solving their own problems, offering creative suggestions to others' impediments or, perhaps better still, being proactive and finding ways to solve things before they become impediments.

The following story, while nothing to do directly with Scrum, is nonetheless relevant to Scrum teams and the ScrumMaster role.

"Good evening folks, welcome aboard Southwest Airlines Flight 372, with service to Oklahoma City," began the flight attendant. "Those of you who have flown us before know that we do things a little differently here at Southwest."

"We're gonna shake things up a little bit. I need a little audience participation or this is not going to go over well at all," he continued.

"All I need is for you to stomp and clap and I'm gonna do the rest—cos I've had five flights today and I just can't do the regular announcement again or I'm just gonna put myself to sleep so…"

The flight attendant then set the travellers off with a beat, "Give me a stomp…clap…stomp…clap…come on…stomp…clap…"

Then he rapped along with the beat:

> This is flight 273 on SWA.
> The flight attendants who are serving you today—
> We've got Teresa in the middle, David in the back.
> My name is David and I'm here to tell you that
>
> Shortly after take off, first things first,
> There's soft drinks and coffee to quench your thirst.
> But if you want another kind of drink then just holla;
> Alcoholic beverages'll be four dollars.
>
> If a Monster energy drink is your thang,
> That'll be three dollars and you get the whole can.
> You gotta pay with cash, we don't take plastic.
> If you have a coupon then that's fantastic.
>
> We know you're ready to get to new places,
> Open up the bins, put away your suitcases.
> Carry on bags go underneath the seat
> In front of you so none of you have things at your feet.
>
> If you have a seat on a row with an exit,

We're gonna come and talk to you so you might as well expect it.
You're gonna have to help evacuate in case we need to;
If you don't wanna then we're gonna reseat you.

Before we leave, our advice is
Put away your electronic devices,
Fasten your seat belt, put your trays up,
Then press the button to make the seat back raise up.

Sit back, relax, and have a good time.
It's almost time to go so I'm done with the rhyme.
Thank you for the fact that I wasn't ignored;
This is Southwest Airlines—Welcome aboard!

The whole plane applauded and cheered this unusual and entertaining version of something that most regular passengers either zone out to or find tedious.

Make Work Fun

In the above example, I can imagine the scenario where the flight crew were moaning about having to do the safety announcement every flight. It's a legal requirement even if very few people listen to it so they don't really have much choice but to do it. They do, however, have a choice about *how* they do it. (You can even watch the video [1] if you want to see the rap in its full glory.) Most Scrum teams also have things that they would rather not do but must. While sometimes great ScrumMasters can help remove the overhead of some of these aspects of red tape, great ScrumMasters can usually help teams find interesting, fun and innovative ways of getting the mundane things done.

Mark Twain said, "Work is what we are obliged to do. Play is what we are not obliged to do." Great ScrumMasters help introduce a playful aspect to work. You can think of this as leveraging the Tom Sawyer effect. In Twain's *The Adventures of Tom Sawyer* [2], Tom is forced to whitewash his aunt's fence as punishment for skipping school. His friend, who is on his way to the swimming hole, sees Tom out working and stops to chat. Tom makes his friend believe that whitewashing fences is such good fun that his friend joins in. Tom continues to pitch the job to the passersby until not only are several of his friends doing the work for him, they are actually paying him for the privilege! What is work to one person can be a great opportunity for someone else; it is often as simple as changing perceptions.

> *"The opposite of fun is not work, it's depression.*
> *We believe work can be fun, and when it is you get more done."*

So write Sam Laing & Karen Greaves, of Growing Agile in South Africa. They blogged [3] about how they turned their admin time into fun time by playing "four in a row" (or Connect 4 as we call it in the UK), with sticky notes denoting their admin tasks. They tell of how once they turned their tasks into a game, they got distracted less often, were more focussed and, as a result, probably doubled productivity in their least favourite aspect of work…and had fun!

Fun Time

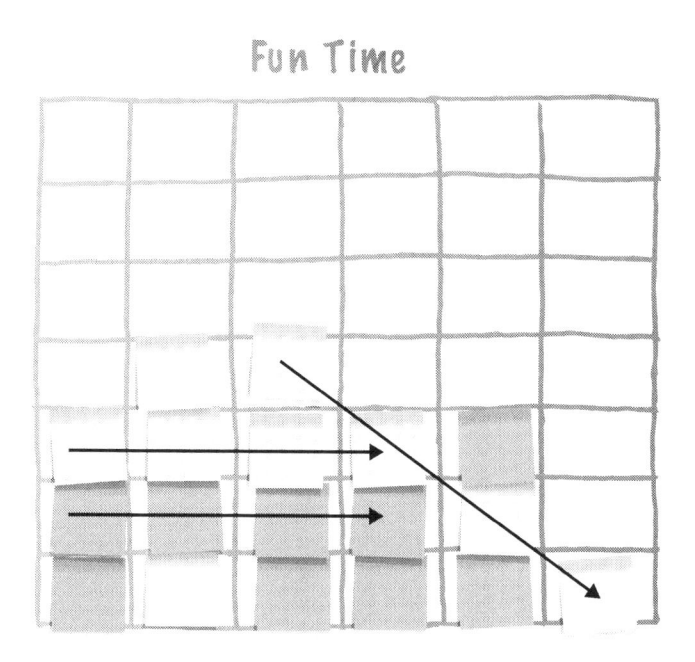

The simplest, most effective way of a ScrumMaster increasing the chances that the team will find creative ways to handle mundane work is to use the sprint to create a safe container where the team can innovate. The ScrumMaster can work with the product owner and management to define business problems that need solving and identify the absolute constraints that teams need to work within. Rather than have a list of solutions they are required to implement, the team then have free rein to solve the problem and meet business needs within those constraints in the most creative way possible.

Remember that teams need space to be creative and proactive— they can't and won't do so if they are overloaded—so ensure your team is working at a sustainable pace. When you do see something innovative happening, make a point of highlighting, recognising and appreciating it to encourage similar behaviour in the future. One simple thing to consider is the amount of work taken into the sprint. The more space a team has, the more creative they are likely to be, so try to leave a little space in each sprint for creative problem solving.

To get people into the practice of being creative, try giving them an alternative medium such as Lego blocks or modelling clay to express their thoughts or ideas. Lego blocks are a great tool to use in sprint planning sessions (to model potential system solutions for example) and retrospectives because they allow people to illustrate their ideas and thoughts. Another great technique for practicing creativity is the improv game of "Delight" [4]. In the game of Delight it is your job to tell someone else's story. Your partner (whose story you are telling) cannot speak except to say "no" to the bits of the story that they don't agree with. The storyteller then must react to this "rejection" by trying something else to make their partner happy with the story. It seems so simple...and it is great fun.

Another way to leverage the team's collective genius and encourage them to solve problems themselves in the future is to include them in the brainstorming process by asking them a powerful question or two, such as:

"How would you like it to be?"
"If you were me what would you do first?"
"What would be your backup plan?"
"If there were absolutely no constraints, what would you do?"
"How could we make this fun or, at least, bearable?"
"What assumptions do we have that might not be true?"

"Remember that teams need space to be creative and proactive"

*"So what do you mean?
Deliver more value without working longer hours?"*

Sprint Goals

A good ScrumMaster helps ensure the high-value product backlog items are selected in sprint planning. A great ScrumMaster helps craft an inspiring, engaging and synergistic sprint goal.

Sprint goals are the forgotten man of Scrum. The early Scrum literature asked for the team to work out what they could do from the product backlog, craft a sprint goal and commit to that goal. Somewhere along the line, however, teams just seemed to forget about the practice of sprint goals and instead just made a commitment to deliver a number of product backlog items. These teams have missed out on so much potential value as a result.

Without question, the most effective, happy and successful Scrum teams that I have seen all make great use of sprint goals. Without them, Scrum teams run the very real risk of turning into a monotonous factory production line and the organisation runs the risk of missing out on the synergies available within the product backlog and the Creativity of their teams.

The following story shows how one team stumbled across the concept of sprint goals and how it helped them deliver more value and a higher velocity.

Greg, the product owner for Team Speedwagon, was pleased with the Release Burnup chart for the last six sprints. The amount of "Greg Dollars" the team had been delivering was really high and had been for the last couple of sprints:

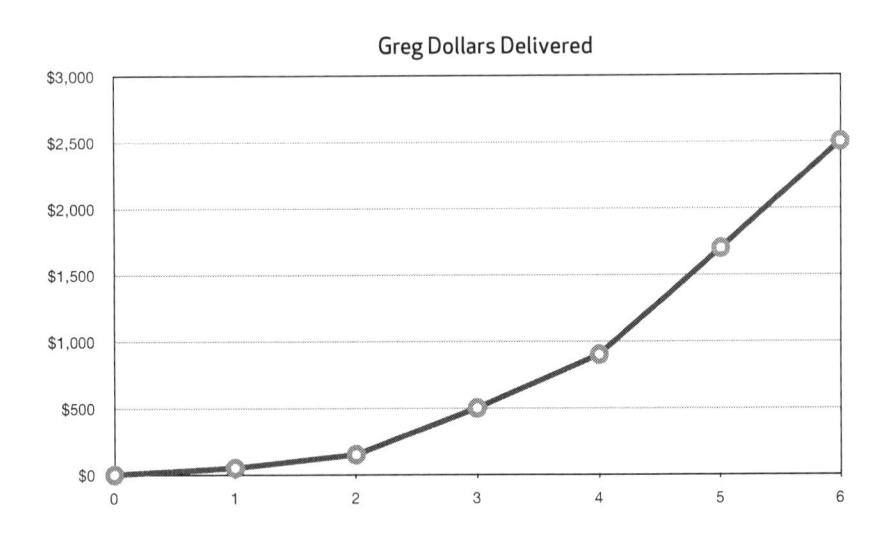

Greg Dollars Delivered

Greg Dollars was a technique for relatively valuing product backlog items that Greg had learned from his product owner training last year. As well as being helpful for him in terms of prioritising the product backlog and quantifying the benefits of each sprint, it also seemed to have a surprisingly positive impact on the motivation of the developers. They seemed to be quite energised by working out how they could maximise the amount of Greg Dollars they delivered each sprint. At the sprint review Greg took the opportunity to show everyone his graph and to point out that sprint 6 was just as successful as sprint 5. The product backlog had been re-stocked and Greg was keen to hear the outcome of the next sprint planning session. In Greg's view, things couldn't be better.

In the sprint retrospective, Spencer (the Speedwagon's ScrumMaster) opened with some data for the team to digest. He posted Greg's value delivered graph on the wall and then put up the velocity burn up graph and the product backlog.

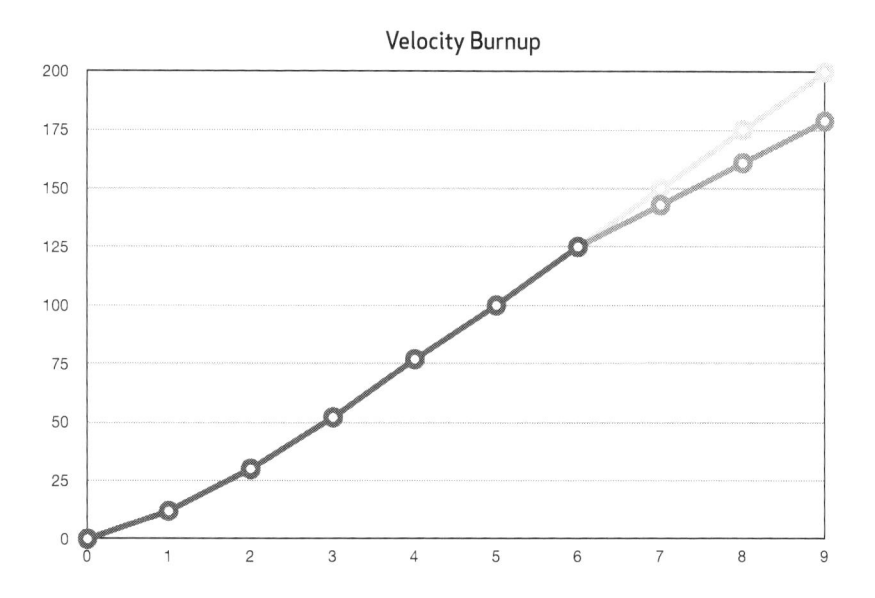

Velocity Burnup

"According to the data, our velocity range is 18-25 points per sprint," Spencer observed. "And, given the composition of the product backlog, it looks like we can do between five and seven of the highest priority items, which would give us somewhere in the region of G$800 for the next sprint. The question that I would like us to focus on for this retrospective is, "How can we increase the amount of Greg Dollars we can deliver in sprint 7 without compromising our sustainable pace?"

The team looked a little confused.

"So what do you mean? Deliver more value without working longer hours?" asked Connor.

"Exactly. And without reducing your quality" added Spencer. "Let's just assume for a minute that it is possible and see if we can find the answer. Break up into groups of three for ten minutes to kick a few ideas around and then we'll come back as a group and share what we've discovered."

When the team came back together, the group of Martha, Laine and Connor suggested that they could convince Greg that some of the items on the product backlog were worth more Greg Dollars than he had initially suggested. They proposed having that conversation with him during sprint planning. There was a chuckle from the rest of the team as they realised that this was a somewhat tongue-in-cheek suggestion.

Connor continued, "I know it's gaming the system and it's effectively cheating but there truly are a couple of items on the product backlog that are to do with removing some of the technical debt. Greg doesn't put much value on these items. If he was aware of how much easier tidying up those areas would make his life and how it increases our ability to deliver his other stuff then he might be willing to put more value on them. This would help us in the short term and, more importantly, in the long term."

"Fair enough," said Spencer. "Finding a way of prioritising the technical debt items would be great, so I definitely think it's worth talking to Greg about. What did the next group come up with?"

Lori, Harry and Ravi had apparently been discussing alternative ways of delivering the high-priority items on the product backlog so as to be more efficient.

Harry summarized it on behalf of his group, "Well, in-keeping with the agile principle of maximising the amount of work not done, we thought we could simplify the designs of a couple of the features to strip out a bit of the complexity, which should then give us extra time to take on a couple more stories."

"Well, that sounds like a good idea as well," said Spencer. "We should run those options past Greg tomorrow and see what he thinks. Personally, though, I can't see a problem with them.

"What about the third group?" he asked, looking at Sian, James and Ben.

"Well, we took a slightly different approach and looked for synergies," Sian began. "We thought that the top three priority features—chat, forum and Facebook link—were all kind of related. So we looked further down the product backlog for other items that were in those areas. By bringing in priorities 7, 8, 11, 12 and 19, we think that we could deliver G$1,000 of value."

"But that's 30 points of effort, guys. We've only ever achieved 25 points before," observed Spencer. "I did say that you couldn't jeopardise your sustainable pace."

"We know that but, because these items are so closely linked, we think that we could actually do them all if they were in the same sprint," claimed Ben.

"I think they are right, Spencer," agreed Connor. "And given that they are all related to connection and chat, it almost looks like the whole sprint could be summed up with the goal, "Getting to know you." He looked at his teammates who seemed to understand and agree.

Lori even started to sing, "Getting to know you...getting to know all about you..." from *The King and I*.

"Interesting," said Spencer. "So are you suggesting that we go to Greg and suggest that, by skipping a group of higher priority items and instead bringing some related lower priority items into this *Getting To Know You* sprint, he could end up with 25% more Greg Dollars than if we just focussed on the highest priority items?"

"That's exactly what we're suggesting," said Sian.

Priority and Value

As a general rule, teams should be pulling items into the sprint from the top of the product backlog (the top items being the highest value items). Good ScrumMasters ensure that teams are able to do this. Spencer and the team had pleased their product owner; Greg felt he was getting good value and receiving his highest priority features. Yet Spencer felt the team could do better and challenged them to discover some ways they could continue to improve.

As counter-intuitive as it may seem at first, teams might find that occasionally taking items from lower down the priority list can lead to a greater overall delivery of value. Great ScrumMasters harness the power of sprint goals both to deliver more value and also to build energy, engagement, creativity and effectiveness into sprints.

Sprint goals can be formed in a few different ways.

Team Speedwagon created their sprint goal bottom up, in that they found a group of related product backlog items that made sense to do together and then worked out what a sensible sprint goal would be for those items.

Some teams prefer to create their sprint goals top down by (usually the product owner) stating a desired future state for the end of the sprint.

The team then choose the items they can bring in to the sprint that will help them achieve that goal.

Both top-down and bottom-up sprint goals can be brilliantly effective. The one approach that I don't recommend, however, is a forced-fit. In a forced-fit approach, the team take the top priority items from the product backlog and then try to define some sort of sprint goal that fits the items. That is usually unsuccessful and often uninspiring because of the unrelated nature of the high-priority items. The result is often a very unconvincing attempt at a sprint goal.

Some teams form sprint goals by writing them in the form of user stories, expressing an actual user need that we would like to satisfy this sprint. Others choose sprint goals from one of the product backlog themes (security, connectivity or "getting scientific" for example). Alternatively I have seen teams make use of metaphors for their sprint goals, such as The Mars Bar Sprint, which originated from the catchphrase "a Mars a day helps you work, rest and play." The team chose this goal to express the fact that, starting with this sprint, they were going to introduce a little bit of technical debt removal and a little bit of fun every sprint, along with the new functionality they had been delivering. Plus the work they were taking on seemed "a little bit chewy!"

There was also the team who created their sprint goals based on celebrities. They had the Paris Hilton Sprint, which was more style than substance; the Nelson Mandela Sprint, which involved some sacrifice for the greater good of the product; and the Lady Gaga Sprint, because they were dealing with a number of somewhat eccentric requests from their stakeholders. A motivating, inspiring and compelling sprint goal is a great example of *purpose*: one of what Dan Pink [5] calls the three elements of motivation 3.0.

In his book, Drive, and his oft-watched TED talk [6], Pink talks about the three elements of motivation in environments where creative thought and cognitively-challenging work is required (and Scrum projects definitely fit that definition):

AUTONOMY
The desire to be self-directing and have control over, if not what you do then, how you do your work

MASTERY
The desire to get better at what you do

PURPOSE
The knowledge that what you are doing has a reason; that it is contributing to something worthwhile and bigger than just the task. A sprint goal definitely fits in to this element of motivation

Other examples of sprint goal metaphors include:

- Sports teams
- Movies
- Song titles or bands
- Animals
- Modes of transport
- Foods
- Countries
- Gadgets
- Advertising slogans

The list goes on and on. Not only can sprint goals have a big impact on the bottom line delivery, but they can also have a huge boost to the energy and motivation of the team.

*Over lunch Henning and Manda
offered to help Mirjam work on the problem.*

Burn The Burndown?

*A good ScrumMaster updates
the sprint burndown to free the team from overhead.
A great ScrumMaster helps the team find a fun way
to manage themselves visually.*

One of the most misunderstood aspects of the Scrum framework, and one of the first things to get dropped in many teams, is the sprint burndown. This simple yet powerful tool that displays quite visibly the state of progress during the sprint is often jettisoned by the team or handed off to the ScrumMaster to deal with. The sprint burndown was intended to be a tool for the self-managing Scrum team to manage themselves during the sprint; to aid them in their daily re-evaluation of their sprint commitments.

In reality though, sprint burndowns tend to be misinterpreted or simply become monotonous, causing the team to either resent their use or find reasons not to use them. The following story shows how one ScrumMaster, Mirjam, attempted to deal with just such a situation.

It was 7:45. Mirjam was at the sprint backlog wall where the team's sprint plan & burndown was visibly displayed. Her first task at the beginning of every workday was always to update the sprint burndown for Team B.O.B. Every night, before leaving, every member of the team updated the tasks he or she was working on that day with the amount of effort remaining. Every morning, Mirjam added the total hours remaining across all tasks and plotted it on the burndown chart so the team could see how they are doing at the start of each day. Mirjam agreed to update the burndown for the team after they had threatened to ditch the sprint burndown altogether if they had to do it themselves.

Though she had agreed to take on the burdensome task of plotting progress, the overhead was even beginning to grate on Mirjam. This morning she thought she would do something about it. During the daily scrum, Mirjam asked the team if they still found the graph useful. When the team confirmed that they did, she asked if anyone could spare any time today to work on a way the team might be able to remove this overhead altogether.

Over lunch Henning and Manda offered to help Mirjam work on this problem. Together, they decided that an electronic supplement might help them. If they created a really simple spreadsheet to mirror the wall, the team members could each update one or two cells in a spreadsheet and have the graph automatically created for them. All Mirjam would have to do was print out the latest version and stick it on the wall each morning.

This worked well for a couple of sprints. It wasn't too long, though, before the team started to get a bit slack in updating the cells in the spreadsheet. It eventually disappeared from the wall completely. One retrospective, Mirjam asked the team about their lack of a visible progress indicator and whether they wanted to try something else instead of a burndown chart.

"Like what?" Henning asked. "I thought that's what you used in Scrum."

"Well, yes. But what if you could find another way to help manage yourselves during the sprint? What would be the harm in that?"

The team split off into a few smaller groups to come up with some alternatives and, after 15 minutes, they presented them to the wider team. One group had simply inverted the burndown chart into a Burn*Up* chart. Though this was not particularly ground-breaking, they seemed keen on the variation. Another group had decided to create a new graph that tracked different types of work items that they worked on during the sprint—features, bugs, changes, etc. Another group suggested a weather-forecast style progress indicator that the team could use to indicate their thoughts on how the sprint was going on a daily basis. The final group suggested that they swap the burndown for a chart showing how many story points had been achieved and marking them with pictures of pints of beer, on a 2-points-per-pint ratio. The idea, they said, was that the more points the team delivered, the more pints they would have at the end of the sprint.

The weather forecast options

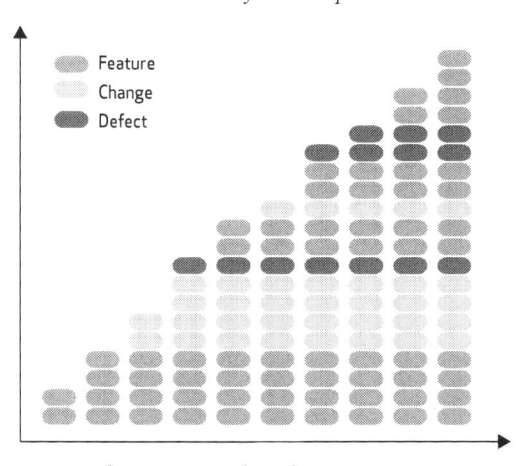

An alternative graph to show team progress

Graph showing the accumulation of story "pints"

The team decided they liked the idea of converting story points into pints and the simplicity of a general feeling about the sprint, so they went for a combination of the pint graph and the weather forecast, both of which the team seemed more than happy to keep up to date themselves.

Misuse of burndowns

The intention behind the sprint burndown is for the team to be able to glance at two lines on a chart and use that data to supplement their conversation about re-planning the remainder of their sprint in order to meet their commitments. However, many organisations see the sprint burndown (and the daily scrum) as a method of keeping track of the team on a daily basis. This quickly feels like micro-management of the team—the exact opposite of the intention of Scrum. We saw something similar in the "Tale of Two Scrums" chapter. The irony is that, if third parties allow the sprint burndown to be used for the purposes of the team, rather than as a micro-management tool, it could become an incredibly valuable information radiator for the rest of the organisation. However, too often, its primary purpose is instead to give information on the state of progress of the team to others. When that happens, not only does the team rebel, but the information is also much less likely to be accurate.

Teams that rebel against the sprint burndown usually are rebelling against the use of the burndown by other parties (perhaps the ScrumMaster or the product owner or even those outside of the direct Scrum team) and will cite a lack of time or unnecessary overhead as an excuse not to continue with the burndown. So while a good ScrumMaster will remove any impediments and reduce the overhead on the team, the great Scrum-Master would reduce that overhead (make it easy for the team to update the burndown or even make it automatic) and also remove any external pressure that may be causing the team to rebel against it.

The Goal Is the Thing

Over time, as the team matures, they may find other, better ways to manage themselves visually. Great ScrumMasters will recognise and encourage the team's greater ownership of their process, even if it doesn't match up exactly to one of the specified Scrum artefacts. The point, after all, is not for the team to draw a graph but for the team to find a way of visually representing their collective progress so that they can effectively manage themselves. The trick is knowing whether they are just looking to avoid the spotlight that it might be casting on them or when the team is actually ready to do this. (Going back to the concept of Shu-Ha-Ri, the team should be in Ha or, even better, Ri.)

As with a number of aspects of Scrum, if teams can find alternative ways of meeting the goal of a part of the framework, ScrumMasters should encourage them to try it.

RETRAI**N**ED

Nurturing

*"We need four hugs a day for survival.
We need eight hugs a day for maintenance.
We need twelve hugs a day for growth."*

Virginia Satir

Don't worry all you conservative Brits out there; I'm not suggesting that ScrumMasters should be huggers! However, the concept of supporting and nurturing the team is key to team growth. As they say, even the grandest of oak trees started as a tiny seed and needed the right conditions for growth, which though tentative and slow at first eventually became a strong, sturdy, immovable object that could withstand almost any conditions.

Great ScrumMasters look upon the team as simultaneously a continual work in progress and a work of wonder with unlimited potential. They want the team to grow, taking a sense of personal pride out of their development as both individuals and as a self-supporting and high-performing unit. They have an almost laissez-faire paternalistic attitude in their approach to team growth. Great ScrumMasters are very protective of the team, ensuring they are not undermined, distracted or sabotaged and, at the same time, ruthlessly encourage the team to self-manage and self-regulate.

This attitude is based on a genuinely positive view of human nature; the belief that very few people turn up to work in the morning thinking, "Do you know what? I fancy screwing up today!" Great ScrumMasters believe that people want to do a good job and that looking for, recognising and building on people's strengths is more likely to lead to their potential for doing a good job to be realised.

At the same time, great ScrumMasters know that sometimes individuals will need to trade-off some of their own personal aspirations for the good of the team. The old adage of "there is no *I* in *team*" is true to a degree but great ScrumMasters balance the fact that, while a great team cannot really tolerate individual self-interest, that team is made up of individuals who all have their own desires, needs and interests.

TIP Facilitate your team to come up with their definition of a great team, drawing from their experiences of great teams in the past. Ask them to spell out the benefits of a great team and what is required both to become a great team and also to maintain that greatness. Look for values and principles that can be applied to any situation as well as specific behaviours that can be applied immediately. A team-values exercise such as the High Performance Metaphor, as described by Lyssa Adkins in her book *Coaching Agile Teams* [1], is a simple yet powerful tool that can be used by great ScrumMasters to help their teams navigate through disharmony to a new level of teamwork.

*"This is getting ridiculous.
Why do I always end up having to pay for your poor quality?"*

The Problem Team

*A good ScrumMaster notices
areas for improvement in the team.
A great ScrumMaster recognises and highlights
strengths for the team to build on.*

Imagine your child brings home a report card with *A*s in Maths, Science, History, and Technology, *B*s in English and French, and an *F* in Geography. Which subject are you most likely to talk to your child about? The chances are it will be the anomaly: the *F* in Geography. We tend to focus on the area with the most room for improvement and this is not necessarily a bad thing. It would not be wise, for example, to simply ignore your child's failing grade. At the same time, though, there is a lot to be said for concentrating on what we are good at and maximising that. Likewise, all good ScrumMasters will help the team reflect on where they can improve, which is a really valuable—if not critical—thing to do. What I have noticed, however, is that the great ScrumMasters, like Paris in the story that follows, focus much, much more on the team's strengths than their weaknesses.

Paris was a bit nervous. After the Christmas break, she would be switching to the Dominos team to replace their ScrumMaster, Nicola, who had recently left the company. Paris had specifically been told that she would be a good influence on the Dominos team, who didn't have a great reputation. Paris had witnessed a few arguments in their daily scrums and had heard the Dominos referred to more than once as the problem team.

On the morning of her first day with the team Paris was walking the floor, looking at the team artefacts on the walls. She noticed that, in addition to the sprint backlog board, the team also had another board. One of the team members, Claire, noticed Paris looking at the board and said, "That's the crapboard. Basically it's all the stuff that we have to sort out because of the crap *some of us* have built in the past." Claire looked pointedly at her teammate Damien.

"Hmmm. Well, it's good that you have captured it all," said Paris, wondering what she was in for.

It wasn't long before she found out. During the sprint planning session, Alison, the product owner, kicked things off by explaining the top priority items she was hoping for this sprint.

"They seem like really valuable items, Alison, but there's no way we're going to be able to do even half of them with all the trash we need to sort out after last sprint's hot fixes," said Claire.

"Well there's a surprise," responded a clearly frustrated and sarcastic Alison. "This is getting ridiculous. Every sprint you guys find an excuse for not taking on work, and it's usually down to something that you did badly last time. Why do I always end up having to pay for your poor quality?"

"We did tell you that we were working on some risky items and we did get them out in time for you," offered Claire.

"Yeah but it's the same old story every sprint. I'm getting tired of it," said Alison looking at Paris. "We need to do something about all these so-called hot fixes."

"I can feel the frustration," said Paris, "I'm still getting up to speed so there's not much insight I can give to the hot-fixing issue at the moment. How about we look at working out what we are capable of for this sprint for now and work from there?"

There was some obvious tension in the room but a grudging acceptance of Paris' suggestion.

"This item here is marked *spike*. How do you normally handle spikes?"

The team explained that the items marked *spike* were ones that the team didn't feel were well understood enough and, as such, needed to be worked on a bit before they could be planned into a sprint. The team went on to say that they didn't worry too much about the low priority spikes, as they had plenty of time before they had to deal with them, but any that had made their way towards the top of the product backlog were either addressed in the sprint planning meeting or in a backlog grooming session sometime during the sprint.

"Could you show me how you would go about that for this item?" asked Paris.

Paris mainly observed as the team discussed the user story in question, gaining clarification from Alison about what the solution might be, identifying different options and the risks associated with them, and remaining focussed on the problem at hand. Also, Paris noticed that every member of the team joined in at some point in the identification of the way forward. By the end of the discussion, the whole team seemed to have a good understanding of the problem and a sensible strategy for addressing it in the upcoming sprint.

As they were wrapping it up, Paris asked if she could offer some feedback. When the team agreed, she said, "I'm blown away, to be honest. That was possibly one of the best examples of a collaborative, self-managing team I have seen in this company."

It took a moment for this feedback to sink in. The whole team seemed to be waiting for the "but…" One of them, Paul, actually asked, "What do you mean?"

Paris explained how each member of the team had contributed to the solution—a hallmark of great collaboration—and how everyone's ideas were amalgamated into something that couldn't be attributed to any one person. She pointed out how impressive it was that the team had taken account of risks and looked for various options before deciding on a route forward.

"And it's obvious that you care about this piece of work. Now, how do you think you could apply this process to the issue of hot fixing?" she finished.

"Well if we had this kind of discussion about each story, rather than just the spikes, then I think we could avoid a number of the problems that we normally run into," suggested Claire.

"Would that be a more useful way for you to spend the remainder of your sprint planning time then?" asked Paris.

The team agreed.

During the sprint, there were a few bumps and intra-team conflicts that needed to be worked through but, by and large, Paris considered this to be a successful first sprint with her new team. To reflect this, she determined that the theme for the retrospective should be "The Awesome-ness Retrospective"

She asked the team to list all of the reasons why being part of the Dominos is good. What makes it enjoyable to come to work, why are they successful and what would they miss about this team if the team were disbanded tomorrow? When they had finished, she posted the answers on the wall. She then asked the team to list all the things that would need to happen for this team to become the best team in the company, the team that everyone would be queuing up to be a part of. This second list became what Paris called their *awesome-ness backlog*.

She asked the team to prioritise this awesome-ness backlog and then select one or two items from it to focus on for the next sprint, with the aim of becoming a little bit more awesome every sprint.

Coach to Strengths to Overcome Weakness

The Dominos had been told so many times what they weren't good at, that they didn't even realise they had the capacity to do good things. Their *problem team* reputation could well have been a self-fulfilling perception. They needed someone to notice what they did well and help them build on success rather than focus on shortcomings.

As coaches, great ScrumMasters help teams tackle problems by asking questions like, "How can we use what we are good at to help us in this situation?" Or "How can our skills and expertise in X make Y easier for us?"

One of the Scrum values is *respect*. Part of respecting people includes holding a generally positive view of human nature. Because we respect our colleagues, we believe that most people want to do a good job. One way of helping ensure people do a good job is by believing in them (See the "BELIEF" chapter for more on this). But beyond that, we must help them believe in themselves if they are to realize their potential and truly become a high-performing team. Your belief in them must be genuine however; if you try to fake your belief in someone, or the team, it will be detected and have the opposite effect on self-confidence. Ensure you pick a credible strength to build upon, one that they can recognize, acknowledge and then visibly use in their path of self-improvement.

It's very easy to go along with the labels that have been attached to people, teams, and even organisations; they can very easily become self-fulfilling. Paris couldn't help her initial preconceived notions—but she dismissed them and purposefully focused on what she saw that day during sprint planning. She noticed the bad, yes, but she chose to focus on the good.

Regardless of where your team is in its development or maturity, I would recommend you consider the technique of a team improvement (or awesome-ness) backlog in retrospectives. It can be a great way to recognise team achievements and help encourage a process of continuous improvement. Great ScrumMasters help teams first of all become aware of their strengths and then decide how to use them to develop even further.

*"How can we use what we are good at
to help us in this situation?"*

"What's happening here, Darren?"
"Something is different. I'm not sure what it is but it is worrying me.

Growing Individuals Or SQUADs?

A good ScrumMaster helps every member of the team grow.
A great ScrumMaster helps the team become a SQUAD.

To improve their teams, all servant-leaders should help ensure that a unique strategy exists for every team member to grow individually. However, ScrumMasters soon realise that growing individuals is only part of the solution; great ScrumMasters also focus on how to grow individuals to the point where they are focused more on the team's success than on their own.

The Spiders team are a classic example of the importance of team growth. The team were in their 5th sprint and had been delivering well so far. During a daily scrum on day 16 of the month-long sprint, the following conversation happened between Earl (developer), Darren (developer) and Lonnie (ScrumMaster):

"I'm still working on the business logic of the account management piece and could do with a little help. I know you have a bit of experience in this area, Darren. Do you have any time?" Earl asked.

"Sorry, Earl, I've just got too much on at the moment," Darren replied.

"OK. How about anyone else?"

The rest of the team looked anywhere but at Earl and remained silent. Lonnie had never seen them so reluctant to help each other before, but she remained silent as well.

"OK. Well I'll just carry on as best I can then," Earl said, looking a little disappointed.

After everyone had a say, Lonnie asked about an item on the sprint backlog that had remained untouched so far in the sprint.

"Does anybody have any plans to tackle the algorithm task soon? It's getting close to the end of the sprint and we said it was a risky task in sprint planning yet nobody has started it yet."

Again, the team was uncharacteristically noncommittal. Lonnie was beginning to get a bad feeling about things and asked Darren for a quick word after the daily scrum.

"What's happening here, Darren?" she asked. "Something is different. I'm not sure what it is but it is worrying me. Between Earl not being able to get help and the high-risk items remaining untouched, it looks like the sprint is at risk. Yet everyone is ignoring it and no one is stepping up to help. If you all have it in hand then that's fine, tell me that I am worried about nothing but I am sensing that you are all leaving it to each other. You were much more of a team in the last few sprints."

"You're right that the algorithm is a risky item, Lonnie. And I think that's the problem at the moment. Nobody wants to take that risk just now," Darren conceded.

"Why not?"

"It's review time. Nobody wants to have his name explicitly associated with failure at this time of year," Darren explained. "There are certain times when it's every man for himself, no matter how much we'd like it to be otherwise."

A Risky Reward

Reward policies in an organisation will, sooner or later, come into the spotlight when teams start using Scrum. Scrum implicitly values team delivery rather than individual delivery and contribution to the team rather than individual performance. This is in conflict with a lot of organisational reward policies and can lead to some dysfunctional behaviour, especially around reward time.

One of my first Scrum teams was going along OK until performance review time came around. It was then that the team realised that the individual objectives and targets in everyone's performance reviews were somewhat contradictory to the objectives of the team as a whole. We took this as a retrospective goal—to remove or at least reduce the conflict—and decided that although we couldn't change the whole company-wide performance management system (certainly not in the short term), we could still take some collective action.

Every member of the team was required to have five personal objectives for performance and development but there was nothing in the system that said they needed to be unique. So we agreed as a team that four of those five would be word-for-word the same in everyone's form and would be focussed on the project goals. The remaining objective would be specific to the individual's own unique development pathway. This worked for us and was copied by a number of other Scrum teams in the organisation (and another organisation as it happens) but wasn't institutionalised across the company—it didn't need to be.

As a ScrumMaster sometimes you need to play by the rules, sometimes you bend the rules and sometimes you need to help write new rules. We couldn't just ignore the performance management process but we could encourage the team to find some common ground that would tick the objectives box while also encouraging greater teamwork. While this is a good short-term fix, great ScrumMasters work with the team to also come up with some pro-active suggestions on how to change the system for the better over the long term.

Make A Hole To Make It Whole

A team cowed by performance reviews is unfortunately not the only reason for a lack of teamwork. Sometimes one or more of the team members is just a not team player. What makes it worse is when the person who just won't buy into the team mentality is the star player.

Whether you look to sports teams or software teams, all highly successful teams have a similar attitude to this situation. Dan Jacobs, in his job as head of talent at Apple famously said, "I'd rather have a hole in my team than an asshole in my team." Jacobs went on to explain that, no matter how indispensable someone may appear to be, you may be surprised how much the rest of the team steps up when that disruptive influence is removed. I couldn't agree more.

Individual growth is necessary for high-performing teams but will only get you so far. The teams that develop the furthest focus on developing both their sense of team and also the strengths of the team as a whole. This is why it is so fitting that *Unity* is the characteristic right at the heart of my SQUAD model, described in *Team Mastery: From Good to Great Agile Teamwork* [2].

I have seen many teams whose environment is discouraging collaboration and encouraging looking out for yourself as individuals. While great ScrumMasters will work tirelessly at changing the environment so that it incentivises more desirable team-based behaviour, they will also help teams reflect on what they want to do about things in the meantime.

Once a ScrumMaster has helped the team develop a strong sense of unity around their identity as a team, they can ask the question:

"Would you rather be materially rewarded for doing the wrong thing or alternatively rewarded for doing the right thing by the team?"

Quite often, comparing the distant, impersonal form of recognition that comes from the corporate objective setting policy is nowhere near as powerful as the feelings associated with successful team-based delivery and individual, heartfelt appreciation given by team members for one's higher-level contribution.

Also, by bringing this question out in to the open, teams will often work out a creative way of enabling each individual to be successful without compromising the team and product level objectives.

"What does a successful team look like?"

Assess Your Way To Maturity

*A good ScrumMaster helps the team develop and grow.
A great ScrumMaster helps the team develop
their own growth pathway.*

So how agile is your team? Are they in Shu? Ha? Ri? How do you know? Should we even care? There seems to be a fairly major split in the agile world between those in Camp A, who believe you need a maturity model, and those in Camp B, who believe maturity models are anti-agile. One thing I am fairly sure of is that traditional maturity models and ways of measuring teams do not map to the world in which agile teams operate—or if they do, they at least reduce the effectiveness of agile teams, which is not the point of these models. I am also sure that almost all maturity models began with good intentions.

I am a firm believer that organisations should not have the aim of becoming agile and neither should teams. The aim of any organisation (and a team) is to be as successful as possible. So, while measuring how strictly you are adhering to the rules and principles of Scrum is not the point, if you believe that an agile approach, such as Scrum, is a viable means of becoming successful then assessing yourself against the application of that framework or process as a proxy metric of success might not be a bad idea.

Most people—and teams are no different, since they are simply a collection of people—yearn to know how they are doing. They are competitive, even if it is only with themselves; they value achievement, growth and mastery. Could we find something that would give teams these factors, and perhaps a little guidance into the bargain? I believe we can. This is a dangerous road though. (I will come back to why it's dangerous a bit later.)

I regularly get asked to help organisations begin their agile journey. Typically this involves someone from the client organisation contacting me and saying something like, "We are moving from a waterfall organisation and need some training in Scrum." As someone who offers Scrum training this is great — I have a customer asking me for one of my products. But is it right for them? My response is always a question about their motivations: "How do you know that you need Scrum training?" or "You are moving from a waterfall organisation, into what exactly?" or perhaps "Why are you moving from a waterfall organisation?" I need to know that they know *why* they are making this change. What are they hoping will be different? Once we know the goal of the organisation we can begin creating a strategy to achieve it and then assess progress against it.

In the early days of Scrum the first maturity model that emerged was the Nokia Test [3] (even though it emerged from Nokia Siemens Networks as opposed to Nokia), where teams were scored against nine metrics to assess how agile they were. As with all first versions there were issues, but it was certainly a useful start for the community that, until then, had nothing. The nine metrics were:

- Iterations
- Testing
- User Stories
- Product Owner
- Product Backlog
- Estimates

- Burndown
- Team Disruption
- Team Ownership

The intention of the test was harmless (and this is key), as its objective was to allow the team to reflect on some characteristics of agile to see where they thought they could improve. And I personally saw a number of teams use the Nokia test effectively; they loved being able to see their progress over time. However, I also saw a number of teams game the system to the detriment of the team, the process and the organisation. For example, if the test values iterations, then it could be implied that the more iterations we have, the better we are. Teams were pushing for one-week sprints, regardless of their capacity and whether it was suitable for the product, just to increase their number of iterations. I saw some teams changing their process to score higher on the test rather than to become more effective. This is a great example of why maturity models are dangerous.

It did however sow a number of positive seeds, for me at least, for team maturity. What if we could tailor the model to encourage more positive behaviour and discourage less dysfunctional behaviour? I began to experiment with a number of the teams I was working with and found not just one model that worked but many. Some teams found measuring themselves against the agile manifesto values to be really effective, some teams found the twelve agile principles to be better for them, while other teams created their own values, principles and behaviours to measure themselves. One team simply used the "awesomeness factor" and asked themselves, "What do we need to do to be the most awesome team in the company—the one that everyone wants to work for and every product owner wants working for them?"

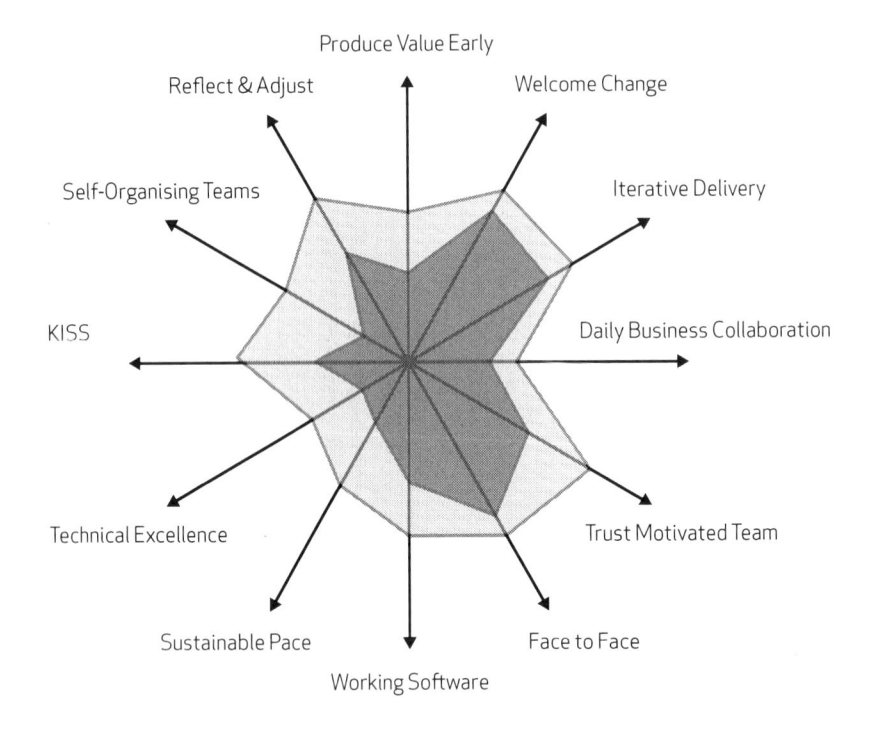

Image of a team mapping themselves against the 12 agile principles over time

In the first edition of this book, I shared a real case study of one team that I worked with to help them define what agile, and success, meant to them. The characteristics that they decided made a team agile and, by proxy, successful were as follows:

CLEAR GOALS
Having a view of the goal of the product, not necessarily the specific detailed requirements

STABILITY
Teams that stay together longer, generally are more productive

SUPPORT
The level of servant-leadership provided to the team

CONTINUOUS IMPROVEMENT
The team's ability and appetite for finding ways to improve their process

SELF-MANAGEMENT
The team's ability to manage themselves and self-organise

ATTENTION TO RESULTS
The team's quality and integrity levels

PREDICTABILITY
How confident can the organisation be in the team's commitments and capacity to deliver

FUN
The degree to which the team enjoys themselves while working

Each of these metrics had levels as well, although no scoring system. For example "Clear Goal" could be broken down to

LEVEL 1: Delivering work with ad-hoc priorities

LEVEL 2: A clear, prioritised backlog but no theme for the iteration

LEVEL 3: A prioritised backlog and iteration theme/sprint goal

LEVEL 4: Sprint goal is part of a release goal with clear customer representation

LEVEL 5: Sprint and release goals are mapped to strategic direction with clear ROI justification

And "Self Management" might be broken down to:

LEVEL 1: The team update the burndown throughout the iteration

LEVEL 2: The team actively utilise the iteration artefacts* to manage themselves
* Note the term burndown has been removed because the team may be using something else (perhaps entering "Ha")

LEVEL 3: The whole team are involved in the decision-making process and own the decisions

LEVEL 4: The team readily critique and explore multiple options before deciding the way forward

LEVEL 5: The team change their process in order to improve; they require no facilitation to manage their own impediments/conflict (perhaps entering "Ri")

Assess Your Way To Maturity

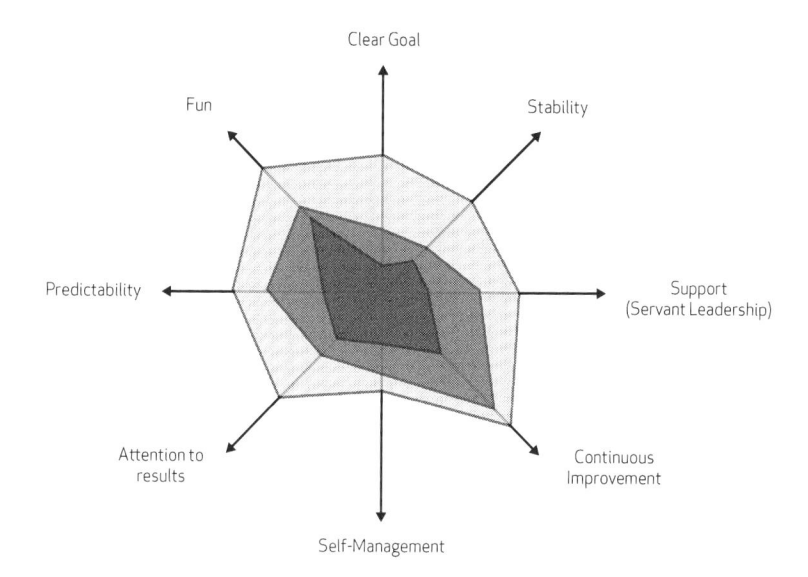

```
              Clear Goal
                 ↑
      Fun              Stability
        ↖            ↗
                              
Predictability ←         → Support
                            (Servant Leadership)

      Attention to      Continuous
        results         Improvement
                 ↓
           Self-Management
```

Image of a team mapping themselves against the above metrics over time

Since then, I have encountered more data points of teams and wrote about it in my 2020 book *Team Mastery: From Good to Great Agile Teamwork* [2]. Here I shared some common characteristics of great teams and 50 milestones that many of them reach on their unique journeys to greatness.

Those characteristics formed the acronym SQUAD:

SELF-IMPROVEMENT
All great teams are constantly looking to improve what they do and how they do it

QUALITY
Great teams take pride in their work and set high quality standards for themselves

UNITY
Members of a great team look out for one another and pull each other onward

AUDACITY
Great teams take risks for the benefit of the team, product and organisation

DELIVERY
All great teams enjoy delivering value and seeing tangible results from their efforts.

In Team Mastery, I introduced the concept of Team Mastery Milestone Cards where the team could celebrate each significant event of team growth whenever they reached it. This is important to recognise the effort and the progress they have made which is all too easily missed in the middle of a busy work life.

However the team choose to measure their own growth and effectiveness is not as important as the environment of wanting to get better…not necessarily more agile but just a better team. If the team are constantly improving as a team, then agility will naturally follow.

"You're on mute, Doug," said Rolo.

Remote Control Scrum

A good ScrumMaster brings team members together.
A great ScrumMaster keeps a sense of
togetherness when apart.

"You're on mute, Doug," said Rolo.

"Sorry," said Doug a little embarrassed. "You'd think by now I would have figured that one out!"

"No worries. You were saying?" encouraged Rolo.

"Thanks. I was just saying that I've never worked with a completely remote team before. I mean, we've always had some people who were based in different offices or different countries or just worked from home quite a bit. But I've never been in a situation where nobody on the team is in the same physical space."

Doug, the team's ScrumMaster, was new to the company having only joined two weeks ago and, after his induction was meeting the other members of The Squirrels for the first time. The rest of the team knew each other a little. Some had worked together but they had never all worked as a team before, and none had been in a situation where everyone was remote from one another.

"I would normally try and get us all in a room together, ideally off-site somewhere, to get to know each other, work out our ways of working and things like that. Then ideally have a bit of a social non-work bonding activity after work. But that's not an option for us, so I'm a little nervous if I'm honest," Doug went on.

"I agree that video-calling is not ideal for getting to know one another but it's definitely our best option right now and, actually it's pretty good these days," said Rolo. "We've got a few tools that we have become quite familiar with over the last few months that allow us to do a lot of the mechanics that we did in physical meetings."

"Absolutely," replied Doug. "I went through them in my induction and they look brilliant. Definitely the next best thing to all being together. In fact, my favourite exercise for getting to know one another would work absolutely fine online I think. If you are all up for it, that is."

"As long as it's not another one of those activities that makes us all cringe with embarrassment," said a team member named Nori.

"It hasn't been the case in the past, Nori, but if at any time you think it's going that way then just let me know. I won't be offended. Also, it's designed so that the cringe-level is totally within your control," Doug said, aiming for reassurance. "In fact, if I go first then you can gauge it before you commit. How about that?"

"Fair enough," said Nori.

Doug then fired up the electronic white boarding software and shared his screen. He then began to doodle, explaining what he was drawing as he went.

"So this is what I call my User Manual. Basically it's like a guide to how I operate, how to get the best out of me and how to troubleshoot me if I start going wrong as it were."

DOUG

SKILLS

WARNINGS

DEFECTS

OPERATING INSTRUCTIONS

Mon-Fre 07:00 - 16:00 SMS Weekends Slow starter

TROUBLESHOOTING

Doug's email suggests he is mad at me
He probably rushed it.

Why is Doug really quiet?
He is probably (a) thinking, (b) tired or (c) leaving space for someone else.

Doug looks upset
He probably feels something he has done hasn't been appreciated or recognised.

SUPERPOWER

KRYPTONITE

231

"My favourite animal is a dog, but my wife is allergic to them so haven't owned one for years. My favourite colour is green and I love almost all kinds of sport and music, although I wish I had a better singing voice!" Doug explained. "I like to think my key skills are my ability to listen, my creativity and the fact that I'm quite brave – or at least other people tell me I'm brave!"

"I'm a little embarrassed to say that I get a bit annoyed at meetings that don't start and finish on time. When people are late I tend to find myself getting a little heated. Also, I've noticed that I have a really strong sense of fairness; so much so that I will actually often find myself arguing for a point of view I don't really agree with if I believe it's not being considered fairly."

Doug went on to explain his preferences for communication medium, working hours and what activities tend to energise him and which ones drain him. He ended by going through a few "troubleshooting tips".

"So if you notice any of these kinds of behaviour from me, then here's the most likely explanation. In the past, people have taken things more personally than my behaviour intended so I thought I would share them with you in advance."

"Wow," said Rolo. "That's really interesting, Doug. Thanks for sharing all of that. Do you want us to do the same?"

"Not strictly," said Doug. "First of all, it's completely optional so I don't want anyone feeling obligated. I'm the new person so I think it's only fair to introduce myself. And secondly, I just chose a few things I thought were interesting, or useful to know. It's not a template in any way."

"So I don't have to do the trouble-shooting bit but I could tell you about my Advanced Life Saving Certification?" asked Nori, smiling.

"Exactly. Whatever you want," said Doug.

The rest of the team then drew and explained their own versions of a User Manual and, despite all of them being different in style and structure, they all managed to share a lot about themselves with their teammates.

"On a scale of 0-10 Nori, how cringe worthy was that after all?" asked Doug.

"I would say a very tolerable 4," replied Nori. "You were right that it was all in my control. What I learned about Tag and Betti was not only useful in the work context but also surprising because I've known them for a long time and had no idea about some things that are quite important to them."

"Well, I appreciate you joining in. It's not surprising to me that you learned something about people you thought you knew. It happens almost every time I run this exercise. It's one of the reasons I love it."

The Squirrels continued their debrief before moving on to planning their first sprint together. They were very explicit in their planning session that they would leave some space for learning to work with one another as this was their very first sprint, and working completely remotely was new to them.

At the end of the sprint, the team used their sprint retrospective to evaluate how things went. As expected things, on the whole, took a little longer than they would have liked but they were actually more productive as a team than they thought they would be.

"I think it's because we actually found some greater opportunities to focus than we had previously. In planning we focussed on all of the noisy but effective collaboration that we would be missing by not being physically together but we didn't account for the benefit of greater quiet time to just get our heads down," suggested Betti.

"Yeah, by the end of the sprint we seemed to get some kind of balance between synchronous communication for when we needed to be creative and collaborative, and asynchronous communication to allow deeper thought and reflection," added Tag. "As a bit of an introvert myself, I have to say I kind of liked that compared to my previous team who all sat together in an open-plan office."

Distributed, or remote, teams tend to find they need to make more conscious effort to get together when they need to when compared to collocated teams; however, the value they gain from each person being able to get on with something without being disturbed should not be underestimated. So long as the team don't let anyone suffer in silence, this can be a great boost for a team.

"I agree," said Doug. "I was really impressed with what you all managed to deliver. Our approach in sprint planning to pick the more independent work items where possible helped with that, I think, as there was less need than normal to collaborate. I'm not sure we're going to be able to be as selective next sprint, though, so is there anything we could try next time to improve our working together even more?" he asked.

There was a period of silence and it seemed to Doug as though everyone looked thoughtful. "How about we go into smaller groups in breakout rooms to discuss for a few minutes then come back?" he suggested.

They agreed and Doug pushed the button to virtually teleport everyone to separate rooms in groups of three. When they came back there were a number of suggestions, the first of which came from Betti.

"Actually what you did there inspired our first suggestion Doug. Putting us into breakout rooms with fewer people allowed us all greater freedom to talk and think so we thought that, next sprint, we could try all being online in one common voice-call but have individual breakout rooms that we could be in when we need to focus. That way we can easily get hold of people if we need to but we also know when someone is focusing and doesn't want to be disturbed."

"I like it," said Tag. "We thought about having two synchronisation points rather than just one to take account of time zone differences and try and ensure we don't go too far off track during the day."

"Like a daily scrum at the start of the day and another at the end of the day. And maybe only ten minutes each rather than fifteen," Rolo explained.

"Those sound like great suggestions," said Doug before nervously adding, "Can I ask something?"

"Sure," said Rolo.

"On a scale of zero to 'someone invading your personal space', how annoying did you find my checking in with you during the sprint?"

"Ha! So you remember that from my User Manual?" laughed Rolo. "I won't lie; I did notice it but I knew you were checking *in* on me rather than checking *up* on me so it didn't bother me. Plus I put it down to you being new and keen! Did you feel you needed to check in on me that much?"

"Not necessarily, but I admit I found it hard not being able to just pick up on things like I would normally do if we were in the office together. And I hate the idea of people suffering in silence when I could be helping so I thought I would rather risk checking in too much than checking in too little."

"Maybe we could try being a little more explicit in how things are going for us so you know without having to ask. Personally I don't mind you checking in on me. It kind of makes me feel…I don't know…appreciated," said Rolo.

The team had come a long way in their first sprint and, while adjusting to being completely remote had brought challenges for them, it had also brought them opportunities. The topics that The Squirrels covered in this retrospective are very common to other teams who have found themselves in a new, more-remote setup.

Principles over practices

As I mentioned in *Above All, Empower the Team*, when a team matures the principles are so much more important than the practices. This is also important when looking at remote teams. Scrum, like many other agile approaches, was originally created based on the ideal of collocated teams.

The idea behind collocation is that teams that work closely together are quicker, communicate more rapidly and tacitly, and collaborate more effectively. All of this is true and, to be honest, given the choice I would still choose a collocated team if I had free choice. However, this is not always an option and has become dramatically less of an option since the Coronavirus pandemic of 2020.

So when adapting Scrum to a remote setting – and it is an adaptation – the practices may need to be altered, but the principles behind the practices are still just as valid (perhaps even more so). In the story The Squirrels took one of the sacred elements of Scrum – the daily scrum – and split it into two events; one at the start of the day and one at the end of the day. The crucial aspect behind this decision was to keep the principles behind the ceremony in play.

One of the most important principles here is frequent intra-team communication around the daily progress towards the sprint goal. The fact that it is no longer fifteen minutes once a day but, in this case, ten minutes twice a day is secondary.

Psychological Safety

Feeling able to change the working practices to enable the team to be and become more effective is key to being able to put principles over practices. And that only comes from a team having a sense of *psychological safety*, a state defined by Kahn [5] as "being able to show and employ one's self without fear of negative consequences of self-image, status or career".

The ability to adapt the process they were using wasn't the only example of psychological safety in the earlier story. During the User Manual exercise, Doug was very explicit in stating that both the exercise itself and the degree of information to be shared would be completely in the control of the team members themselves. Doug also went first both to demonstrate the exercise and also to increase people's comfort levels with what was being asked of them. He also wanted to set the tone in terms of vulnerability.

Doug also broke the retrospective up into smaller groups in private break out rooms when he sensed a certain level of unease. Working in smaller groups tends to increase psychological safety as there are fewer people to potentially judge each person's ideas. When we bring the ideas back to the bigger group, they are our ideas; there's safety in numbers.

Rolo also demonstrated what I call *continuous positive regard* when Doug asked about his level of checking in. He naturally assumed Doug was acting positively (being keen in a new job, checking *in* rather than checking *up*). If I know that my colleagues are assuming me to be acting positively and if I choose to interpret their actions positively then I feel safer. This is even more important when working remotely.

Great ScrumMasters work tirelessly to create a sense of psychological safety within the team because they know that teamwork will simply be stifled if we cannot trust one another or the environment we are working within.

Remote First is the New Normal

Even before the pandemic, the fully collocated team was the exception rather than the norm. True, those collocated teams often (but not always) had productivity, creativity and other benefits over more distributed teams. However, there are other benefits to being remote – as discovered in our story above – and these often come as a surprise. This is arguably because of the prejudice that when we believe collocated teams to be more effective, it becomes a self-fulfilling prophecy. We have previously never designed our organisations or teams to promote what has become known as *remote first*.

Remote-first as a concept asks us to re-imagine everything we do. Normally, we might think "how can I enable someone who is working remote to participate in my meeting"? A remote-first approach would challenge us to design the meeting as if it were going to be happening completely remotely and then think "how could this be adapted if some people were in the same location"?

This remote-first approach not only helps us cope with remote work but actually allows us to leverage it. We can now attract talent that would previously have avoided joining an office-based, 9-5 company because it would have meant a three-hour round-trip commute. We not only allow our more introverted people to flourish more but allow for a greater work-life balance all round.

Maximise the amount of tools not needed

Molood Ceccarelli, CEO of Remote Forever and someone who has been speaking about the inevitable increased remote nature of agile teams for many years, noted one of the barriers to effective remote working is our magpie-like tendency to accumulate a suite of technological tools that can quickly become overwhelming. In homage to the agile manifesto, she likes to say that ScrumMasters, and other leaders, should help teams "maximise the amount of tools not needed" – I love this quote!

There are other downsides to more remote working too. A greater reliance on technology can easily lead to *screen fatigue*, where we get tired easier. We can feel uncomfortable with our colleagues seeing into our homes and we are more likely to overwork when the boundaries between work and home life are blurred so much.

Whether we are in-person in a single office, spread all around the world, or in some kind of hybrid-distribution in between, great teams see themselves as more than just colleagues. There's no denying that there needs to be greater conscious investment in the social side of things to build bonds, understand one another and avoid suffering in silence. From virtual happy hours to water cooler breakout rooms to bring your dog to work…great ScrumMasters will nurture great teamwork so that we build and keep a sense of togetherness no matter how far apart the team is physically.

RETRAINED

Empathic

*"Most conversations are simply monologues
delivered in the presence of witnesses."*

Margaret Millar

Empathy, according to Wikipedia, is "the capacity to recognise emotions that are being experienced by another sentient or fictional being."[1] One of the best ways to have and show empathy is to listen. True listening is much harder than people think and is a skill that requires practice.

Stephen Covey [2] claims that most people do not listen with the intent to understand; they listen with the intent to reply. ScrumMasters listen to what is being said, what is being implied and also what is not being said. Great ScrumMasters also listen in a way that helps those they are listening to understand as well.

Great ScrumMasters help their teams develop a talent for listening and empathy as well. Imagine the daily scrum for example. In a team of seven people, each person will be listening for significantly longer than they will be talking so the more that each team member can develop their abilities to listen and truly understand, the more effective that team will become.

While ScrumMasters and team members may not necessarily agree with everything they are hearing, by displaying a genuine understanding for a person's beliefs and feelings, they are more likely to increase their relationships with others, resulting in higher levels of collaboration and performance.

> **TIP** To develop your ability to listen and concentrate, sit in a noisy place (perhaps a coffee shop or a park) and try to isolate certain noises - a bird chirping, the sound of the traffic, the wind - and practice blocking out everything but that noise. Don't get discouraged when your mind wanders; that is normal. When it happens, consciously bring your focus back to the chosen noise. Then practice shifting your attention consciously from one noise to another and back again.

If I were to recommend one skill for ScrumMasters to practice it would be empathic listening. It is crucial and has a huge impact on team performance, dynamics, morale and progress.

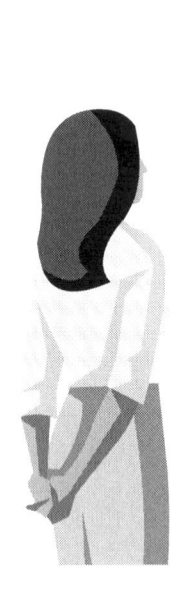

Diane congratulated them on all their hard work and then surprised them with a new challenge

Two Ears, One Mouth

A good ScrumMaster facilitates cooperation between people.
A great ScrumMaster facilitates collaboration.

Cooperation and collaboration are both *good* things but they are not the same thing. You can't get collaboration without at least a degree of cooperation. However, just because people are cooperating does not mean that they are collaborating.

You can cooperate under duress but you can only collaborate freely. When teams collaborate, they build on top of one another's ideas in a "yes, and..." style. Lyssa Adkins describes collaboration as something where "each person gives away their cherished vision of what it 'should be' so that something better, something that none of them could have imagined alone, can emerge" [3] and she quite rightly points out that this type of behaviour requires courage and vulnerability.

Scrum asks people from different departments, with different cultures and skill-sets to work together as a cross-functional, self-managing team. Sometimes the User Experience (UX) or Business Analysis (BA) people have worked no closer than at arms length from the developers but now we are throwing them in the same room and asking them to get features "done" in a sprint. Learning to cooperate with others is hard enough; learning to collaborate with them takes serious time and effort.

The first step, and it is by no means easy, is to get these various people to simply cooperate with one another; get them to work together for the common good of the team and the project. The second step is to begin to break down any barriers between roles, functions, or personalities and build a cohesive, cooperative team.

For an example, let's look at a story. Diane's team was co-located and cross-functional; they had no major teamwork issues yet the team just wasn't collaborating as Diane knew they could. Each person was focused on the task at hand and rarely asked for, or offered, help. Diane did a little research and came to the next sprint retrospective prepared to propose a different kind of team building activity.

The sprint retrospective went well. Diane mentioned at the start that she would like to challenge the team to come up with better ways to collaborate. The team came up with some ideas, including pairing and regular "whole-team" design sessions, which they were excited to try. At the end of the sprint retrospective, Diane congratulated them on all their hard work and then surprised them with a new challenge.

"All of your ideas are good ones and I'm excited to see you put them into action during the next sprint," Diane began. "I want to suggest an additional activity. I've been reading about improv theatre. It is said to be the most pure, natural and direct example of collaboration. To help us move to that next level, I want us to go out as a team to the local comedy store for an improv night and see if we can pick up any tips."

After the giggles subsided, Diane explained that an improv team have no script and have to respond to unpredictable stimuli...as a team. When one member of the team speaks, rather than think "why did he say that?"

or "what a terrible idea," another team member immediately builds on the direction the first teammate has taken (choosing to believe that the suggestion was both inevitable and inspired) and attempts to add something to it in order to further the team's objectives. If one of the team is struggling, another teammate will come to the rescue instantly.

Though the team moaned and groaned a bit, in the end they all showed up. By the end of the evening, not only had they shared a good laugh and increased their bond outside of work but they had also decided to experiment with some of the fun improv games back at the office to help develop their team's collaborative spirit and skills.

In fact, the team enjoyed the games so much that they decided to change their team name from the Sonics to the Sonic Players in homage to their increased collaboration skills and love of improv theatre!

Intuition and Improvisation

Intuition is an important skill for a ScrumMaster to invest in and develop. Though things on the team were OK, Diane was sensing something unspoken that indicated the team weren't really functioning properly. She chose to act on this intuition both by encouraging the team to propose some in-sprint activities and also by bringing them out of the office to work together outside of their daily project.

If an improv night is too much for your team, you might consider improv games that you can play in the office (or at a local pub). Games such as "one-word storytelling" [4] or "the three-headed expert" [5] or "story spines"[6] are really quick and easy (and fun) games that can help teams get into the mindset of collaboration and practice that skill.

Listen Up

Improv actors and collaborators are all good listeners, a skill every member of a Scrum team should work to foster. In the early stages of Scrum, communication should be established within a team and with the organisation. The team will probably need to make use of many more communication channels than they were previously used to and most likely at a much broader frequency, so encouraging people to talk to each other is a noble and worthwhile aim. Usually the most obvious example of this is at the daily scrum, where the purpose is for team members to share their status with their colleagues and use that information to re-plan on a daily basis.

The old adage of "you have two ears and one mouth so use them in that proportion" comes to mind. During a daily scrum for a team of seven (Scrum's ideal team size), everyone is listening to talking at a ratio of roughly 6:1. And I don't just mean hearing the words that people speak but actively listening to the words, the tone and the intent so that we know if our teammates are OK or whether they need help. This brings to mind another good-to-great truth:

> *A good ScrumMaster encourages people to talk to each other.*
> *A great ScrumMaster encourages people to listen to each other*

As I mentioned previously, listening is a skill that can, and should be, developed. There is a distinct difference in energy within a team who are actively listening to one another and a team that are waiting for someone to stop speaking so that they can have their turn. Another really simple (and fun) exercise that you can try to help your team really listen is "First Letter, Last Letter."[7] . The only rule to the game is that the person who speaks must start their first word with the last letter of the last word of the previous speaker. For example:

"…The only impediment I have got is that I have a departmental meeting to attend this afternoon."

The next speaker must therefore begin their sentence with the letter 'n', for example:

"Naturally…yesterday I was working on…"

You can also try changing up the order of who talks next with a ball that is thrown from person to person to help ensure that everyone is listening to what *each person* is saying, not just what the person standing next to them is saying.

"I took some notes about how each person either blocked or helped the problem-solving process, whether intentionally or not."

Yes, But That Will Never Work

*A good ScrumMaster
helps teams use "yes, but" effectively.
A great ScrumMaster helps teams
find more space for "yes, and."*

Right from Scrum's introduction, the concept of *yes, and* has been taught as an important mindset for teams, organisations and ScrumMasters. When we first heard about "this agile thing" when I was at BT, there was a fairly broad response of "Well, obviously I can see how it would work in Silicon Valley at companies like Yahoo! **but** it can't work here." And then somebody said, "Well actually, we have tried it here, **and** it worked pretty well."

To which the response was "Yeah, well I can see how it would work in that small project **but** it wouldn't work on an infrastructure project." Even with all of the *buts*, we decided to take this as a challenge to make it work rather than an excuse not to do it. We gave it a try. And guess what? It worked OK. To which someone replied, "Well I can see how it would work on THAT kind of infrastructure project, **but** it wouldn't work if half your project team was in India." And so it continued.

Yes, but is a very common default response to a problem or change. *Yes, but* comments can be incredibly valuable, if used in the right way (i.e. to look at alternatives and to raise risks). So a good ScrumMaster will help teach teams how to use *yes, but* effectively in their process of self-management. At the same time, *yes, but* responses can also stop a team from trying something new or contributing new ideas. That's why great ScrumMasters help agile teams purposefully turn their *yes, but* thoughts into an *offer* or a *yes, and* response.

To see the difference between *yes, but*, an *offer*, and *yes, and* responses, let's follow the Bullet Dodgers during a daily scrum. The main players are Donna, the ScrumMaster, and Jim, a team member with a problem he feels is unsolvable. Watching and taking notes is a consulting coach they've brought in for some advice. Her name is Sarah.

During Jim's turn to share his progress, he said, "As you know I've been working on the download carousel task for the last day or two and I'm pretty much there but I can't fully test it so I'm going to move on to the next item on the board."

"Why can't you test it fully?" asked Donna.

"Because we can't upload the assets to the test environment. It takes too long," explained Jim. "It's been like this for weeks now. It takes four hours to run and we can't do anything while it's running."

"Yeah, I know it's a pain. I've been hassling the guys in Ops to sort it out for us and bring the time down. I'd really like to find a way around it though, in order to meet our commitment to our definition of done, "said Donna. "Could we get Dave to knock up a mirror environment for us?"

"Yes, but I'm not sure how long it would take and it wouldn't really solve the problem for us. In fact, it might make things even more complicated," said Jim as he moved to grab the next item on the board and move it into the "in progress" column, signaling that the conversation was closed.

Sarah, who was quietly taking notes for future discussion, wrote, "*Jim: Yes, but. Blocks the constructive suggestion without offering another.*" Sarah remained silent as the discussion continued.

Donna turned to the rest of the team and asked, "What does everyone else think?"

"Well, I agree that a mirror environment won't solve all of our problems, but it would be an improvement on our current situation. Plus, it would free us up a little to perhaps look into the automation of the build process," suggested Martin.

Sarah again made a note: "*Offer. Agrees with Jim, but suggests another point of view that could move the team forward.*"

"Automation is a nice idea, Martin," said Jim. "But I can't see how we can get it down to a workable turnaround time. You are the only person who knows how to do that and you have a load of other commitments for this sprint," said Jim.

Donna looked at Sarah, who smiled but remained stubbornly silent. "*Another yes, but reply from Jim,*" she wrote. "*Remind them that yes, but replies not only block the team but also reduce morale and teamwork. Knocking down a person's suggestion makes them less likely to offer one in the future.*"

Donna sighed inwardly but kept stubbornly pushing the conversation forward. "Yes, it will be tough, and I know Martin is the only person we feel comfortable touching that part of the code base," she acknowledged. "But I think it's become such a big issue for us that I think I could make a case for us to tackle it head on."

Sarah wrote, "*Donna counters with* offer."

"Yes, that would be helpful, Donna," said Sean enthusiastically. "And I could probably take on some of Martin's remaining tasks in the sprint, if he can help me a bit."

Sarah made a mental fist pump and wrote, "*Sean offers first* Yes, and *response.*"

"I can definitely help you out, Sean, and if we pair up, I think it would also be an opportunity for you to learn about the build process as well," replied Martin. "I know it's a big job but I think it's reasonable to expect that we can get the build running automatically overnight within a few days time."

Sarah smiled as she wrote, "Yes, and *response from Martin. Takes Sean's offer and adds extra value to it.*"

After the team left the meeting to start the day, Sarah stayed behind for a moment to talk to Donna. "Donna, you and the rest of the Bullet Dodgers team addressed a big issue here and, in the process, managed to exemplify an important behaviour of a successful, collaborative team: *Yes, and.*"

Sarah briefly explained the difference between *Yes, but*, *offers* and *Yes, and* to Donna. She then said, "I took some notes about how each person either blocked or helped the problem-solving process, whether intentionally or not. I'd like to bring this up at the retrospective and suggest some ways we can all be more aware of having a *Yes, and* mindset."

"Sounds like a great plan," said Donna. "Let's do it!"

The Power of Collaboration

What really sets the great teams apart from the good teams is that they all use *yes, and* frequently. When teams adopt a *yes, and* mindset, they quickly recognise an offer from one of their teammates and build on it—this is the essence of collaboration and creativity. They find solutions to problems, ways around impasses and take solutions to another level.

A *yes, and* mindset is the basic building block of collaboration and, as we discussed in the previous story, improvisational theatre. Improv actors don't know what is going to come up, but whatever does come up, they are determined to accept, respect, and add to it. Surprising results emerge when we have a *yes, and* mindset in the team; nothing is impossible, nothing can stop us, and the creativity and energy is immense.

Developing a *yes, and* mindset can just be as simple as practicing the concept by starting the daily scrum with an improv game such as "one-word storytelling" [8] to get the team into the habit. You can also try taking on an alternative phrase such as "what I like about your suggestion is…I would add to it by…"

"So what can I do?" asked Annika. "I'm genuinely worried about my career prospects if I say we can't do it but deep down I'm sure it's unrealistic."

Coaching for Change

A good ScrumMaster changes people's minds
A great ScrumMaster helps people change their own minds

In the earlier story *A Tale of Two Scrums*, Stephanie had been trying to create a buffer between Annika the Product Owner and the rest of Team Icarus. She had good intentions but it inevitably led to problems in terms of trust and collaboration. Luckily, it was caught quickly and the relationship grew.

Stephanie managed to explain why they were afraid of giving Annika the real message and how they would all benefit from creating an environment of trust and safety to be transparent about progress. Thankfully, Annika could see the benefits to the product (and therefore her job as Product Owner) to seeing the true state of progress rather than a more palatable but ultimately false message.

Within very little time, Team Icarus were able to spend less energy on managing Annika and more energy on the delivery. This resulted in greater speed, quality and predictability of delivery.

As Annika's product began to get more attention within the business, her boss, the head of product naturally took more of an interest. After a recent 1-2-1 between Annika and her boss Jean, Annika called Stephanie via video call.

"Hey, Steph, how's it going? Have you got a few minutes?" Annika asked.

"Sure, what's up?"

"I've just been speaking to Jean and I think I need your help."

"OK. What kind of help?" Stephanie asked.

"Well Jean is not keen on Scrum at all and wants me to give a presentation to justify why we are using it and not sticking to our 'tried and tested' ways of delivery," she said.

"I have to admit I'm a bit surprised by that," said Stephanie. "I know we had a bit of a rough start but I thought things were going really well."

"They are," Annika said, "but that might actually be a part of the problem. Jean has a big idea for next quarter and wants us to hit a target I don't think is achievable. When I explained the predictable capacity of the team, Jean said that I'm being too soft on them and they have become too complacent."

"Ah. I think I've heard that story before. The 'teams need a higher target to be motivated to continuously improve' story?" Stephanie asked.

"Pretty much. You managed to convince me to try Scrum so I was hoping you could use your powers of persuasion on Jean as well."

"I'm flattered that you think I'm some kind of master influencer, Annika, but I don't have any Jedi mind tricks I'm afraid," Stephanie responded, feeling a little guilty at not helping her colleague out. "And I don't really think I'm the right person anyway because I don't think Jean would consider me to be neutral. As far as Jean is concerned, I'm on the team's side and, to Jean, I am probably one of the reasons they are being complacent. You're from the same tribe as Jean and have a level of empathy and neutrality that I don't."

"So what can I do?" asked Annika. "I'm genuinely worried about my career prospects if I say we can't do it but deep down I'm sure it's unrealistic."

"Well I don't know about you but I tend to operate on the principle that I can't change anyone else's mind, they can only change it for themselves. And they are only going to do that if they see significant benefit and little downside in doing so. Perhaps you could help Jean do a bit of a cost-benefit analysis of the situation?" suggested Stephanie.

"I've kind of tried already. Won't you give it a go? Please?" pleaded Annika.

"I think you underestimate your ability to influence Jean yourself," said Stephanie. "If you could get to the point where you could influence Jean yourself, would that be preferable to you than me influencing Jean?".

"Well, yes, but I've told you I don't think I can."

"OK well so long as you agree that it's a desirable outcome, we can work together on getting you to a point where you think it's possible. Would you like me to coach you on this?" asked Stephanie.

Annika agreed.

"So I just want to clarify what your goal is. What specifically do you want to achieve?" asked Stephanie.

"I want to convince Jean that the target for the next quarter is unrealistic and we shouldn't be pushing the team to commit to it," said Annika, before adding with a smile, "Without losing my job or career prospects!"

"OK. I don't actually think your career is in jeopardy but you know Jean much better than me so let's assume that's a possibility," said Stephanie. "And you told me that you communicated exactly that message but were told you were being too soft on the team and that they have become complacent. What else have you tried already?"

"Nothing yet. Apart from asking you to help," replied Annika.

"OK. I know you have been successful for a while and you can't have gotten to where you are now in your career without changing people's minds. How have you tended to work things like this out before?" Stephanie asked.

"Hmm," Annika thought. "I would say I tend to focus on logical arguments really. Looking at facts and figures, making a case that way and appealing to their intelligence."

"That sounds reasonable. Does it work?"

"Sometimes. Other times people will stick to their opinion despite overwhelming evidence. In those situations, I just tell myself I had no chance to begin with and just move on," Annika said.

"I've had similar experiences myself. It's almost as if the more data you show those people, the stronger their resistance to changing their minds!" laughed Stephanie.

> *"Faced with a choice between changing one's mind and proving there is no need to do so, almost everyone gets busy with the proof."*
> J.K. Galbraith

"I know, right?! Unfortunately, I have a feeling that Jean is one of those people."

"Tell me a bit more about Jean." Stephanie said.

"Well. Jean is a bit of a perfectionist and a stickler for quality. They hate risk and waste. When things get tough, Jean typically likes to take control and get things done their way."

"Interesting," said Stephanie. "It sounds like you know enough about Jean to move to the bottom of the SPEED model [9]."

"What's the SPEED model?" asked Annika.

"Well, there are different ways one can try and coach others to change and, in my experience, it's largely a case of picking the appropriate tactic for the situation," Stephanie said while sharing her screen and drawing on her electronic whiteboard software.

*S*UGGESTIONS
*P*ROOF
*E*NABLERS
*E*NVIRONMENT
*D*RIVERS

"Sometimes offering suggestions or showing data are both really quick ways of getting a response and they can work," Stephanie went on. "But they also can have the opposite effect, as we have both found in the past."

"Sometimes enabling people or influencing the environment can help but the strongest change is usually driver-driven. And you've told me a few of Jean's drivers are quality, risk, waste, perfection and control."

"How could you leverage Jean's drivers to make backing Scrum more attractive and natural?" asked Stephanie.

"Wow. Good question," said Annika.

"When we look at waste, I can see now why there might have been some resistance. So far Jean has seen Scrum as very wasteful because some of our iterations have required us to undo or throw away some of what we did before. But I see that as avoiding the big wastes we have had in the past—things like resolutely sticking to and delivering our original plan even when things have changed," she continued.

"Is there anything you can do about that?" asked Stephanie.

"Well, if I can point out how Jean has saved the company so much money and time by using Scrum to avoid those big end-of-project failures, then that's not so much changing their mind as congratulating their open-mindedness," said Annika.

GROW the change

In the story above, Stephanie adopted a coaching stance with Annika. The first thing she did was ask for permission to coach. Because a ScrumMaster can wear many different hats, great ScrumMasters tend to be transparent about which role they are adopting and don't go around "inflicting their help" as Esther Derby would call it. [10]

Stephanie also made use of two coaching models, the first of which was the GROW model. [11]

She established Annika's **Goal**, then clarified her **Reality** (some facts about the situation, including what she had already tried) before identifying and evaluating **Options** she could take (explicitly asking her what else she could think of before introducing the SPEED model). Finally, she tested her **Will** to take an action and move her situation forward.

Annika and Stephanie both had experience of facts not always winning people over. This is a strange but common factor of humanity. We tend to be convinced by feelings rather than facts. This brings us to the second coaching model that Stephanie used: the RAMEN model [12]:

The RAMEN Model

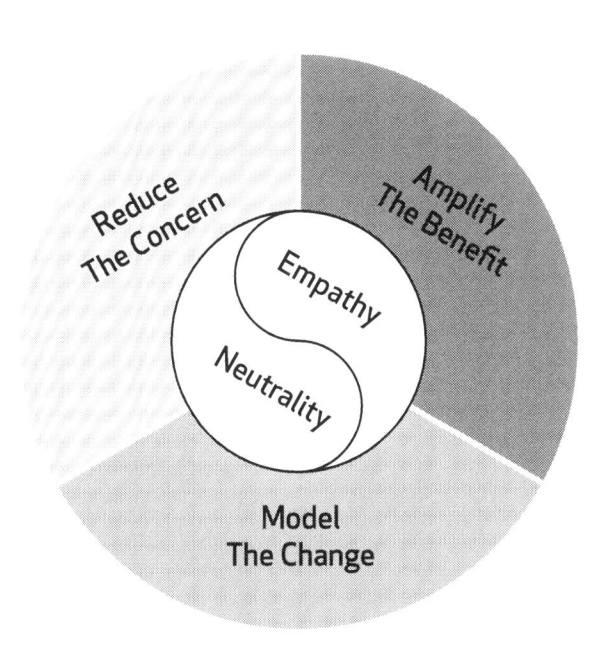

Stephanie knew that in order to coach Jean, she would need to have a relationship with Jean so that they could tap into neutrality and shared empathy. Annika, on the other hand was in the same tribe as Jean and so was much better placed to act as a coach. What Stephanie did was help Annika empathise more with Jean—to empathise with what Jean had to lose and to gain from reconsidering their views on Scrum.

By identifying Jean's values and helping map the options against those values, Annika put herself in a position to coach Jean to possibly change their own mind without fear of losing face or increasing waste. In fact Annika was able to turn these factors into positives for Jean.

In my experience, people make decisions to change so long as the benefits to them of the outcome or change outweigh the costs to them or concerns they have with it. I call this the "change equation". To explain the change equation, I will borrow from my book *Team Mastery: From Good to Great Agile Teamwork* [13]:

When considering taking on a challenge or embarking on a change, everyone calculates their own change equation. It is a simple equation but one that, when understood, can be consciously altered to significantly increase our chances of success.

The equation looks like this:

B* x *P* > *C

Where:
B = *the benefit to me*
P = *the probability of success*
C = *the cost to me*

Let's say, for example, that I am considering getting fit. There are a number of costs to this, including the financial cost of joining a gym or buying equipment, the emotional cost of getting up early to exercise, and the opportunity cost of not being able to eat and drink what I want when I want to. If I can identify the costs then I may be able to proactively reduce those costs somewhat.

There will, hopefully, be benefits to me getting fit – or why would I bother? For example, I might live longer, be able to do more sport, and reduce my health insurance premium. Identifying these benefits may help me realise just how valuable this idea is to me.

Finally, we come to P. There is always a chance that whatever we attempt will not work. So even if the chances of success are 99%, simple mathematics will say that if the benefit and cost are equal then factoring the inevitable chance of failure will lead to people to say no to the change. Put another way, when the benefits (multiplied by the probability of success) do not exceed the cost, the answer is usually no.

100 * 99% < 100

There is one more problem. Even if we factor in the chance of failure and the left-hand side of the equation is larger than the right, we still might not take the chance.

Most of us are loss and risk averse, so we tend to take a pass on opportunities that are only marginally likely to succeed. The endowment effect [14] suggests that we place an unnaturally high value on anything we currently own, and our status quo is such a thing. Because of this, we require a significant return on our risk to justify taking a gamble.

> *"The way to get things done is not to mind who gets the credit of doing them."*
> Father Strickland

Continuous Positive Regard

It's rare to find someone who isn't trying to do what they think is the right thing. Most people act rationally within the constraints of their perspective and experience. So, if we see a dysfunctional behaviour, then the rational explanation for it is that it is usually a symptom of a need not being met or of a value being threatened.

If we can help people meet that need in another way or reduce the perceived threat to that value then we have a greater chance of enabling a more functional behaviour. The "cost" of changing one's mind – or behaving differently – has been reduced. Another cost to changing one's mind is the possibility of "losing face" or being seen as admitting one was wrong in the first place.

Annika avoided this by framing her argument as an opportunity to amplify one of Jean's values and the value add to the company. This may be seen, by some, as manipulation, which is a concern to many ScrumMasters.

A ScrumMaster is a Politician

Because the ScrumMaster is an organisational change agent, they will be required to get involved in organisational politics in many ways. Understanding how people make decisions, change their minds, form alliances and what ambitions and fears they have is a valuable skill to develop. Nurturing a new organisational culture and processes requires skills in organisational politics.

Unfortunately, for many the word politics has become a dirty word but it doesn't need to be. I like this definition of organisational politics [15]:

Organisational politics is the process of using an informal network to gain power and accomplish tasks to meet a person's wants or needs. Organisational politics may be a positive practice when the greater good of the company is affected. However, it can also be negative when people promote self-interests.

Influence and persuasion are fine. Manipulation is not. The difference is the neutrality of intent on behalf of the ScrumMaster. Great ScrumMasters don't pursue their agenda but rather focus ruthlessly on the agenda of those they are coaching and, more importantly, the organisation as a whole.

RETRAINED

Disruptive

*"But nobody else is gonna put it right for me.
Nobody but me is gonna change my story.
Sometimes you have to be a little bit naughty."*

Lyrics from "Naughty" in Matilda The Musical

This attribute is somewhat of a controversial one – as is the quote on the previous page – so bear in mind our other characteristic of Tactful! I remember back to when I first started in the role of ScrumMaster. After a while, my boss told me that he knew that I was doing a good job because I was being "a right pain in the neck." (OK, he used a stronger word than neck!) When I asked him what he meant, he told me that I constantly challenged the reasons why we do things the way we do them and never accepted the answer, "Well that's just the way we do things around here."

Challenging the status quo is a big part of the ScrumMaster role. Any fledgling Scrum team will initially be operating in a legacy environment—one that wasn't set up for Scrum teams. Sooner rather than later they will bump up against the rough, non-agile edges of the organisation. It is here that the ScrumMaster will need to ask, "Why do we do this? Is there another way?"

In the early stages, the ScrumMaster's focus is to help the "alien" Scrum team survive in the host organisation. Soon, though, the ScrumMaster's attention must shift to changing the host organisation so that it not just tolerates Scrum teams but actively supports them. The ScrumMaster, in effect, must help create a new "way we do things around here;" one that is specifically designed to complement Scrum teams rather than the old way of working.

There is a fine line between disruptive and annoying. To be effective you must find ways to defend the team without alienating those *outside* the team. Respect and tact are very helpful in making a point without getting people's backs up.

TIP Work with another ScrumMaster to practice making a case for change on something small and relatively inconsequential. Take time to prepare. What are the facts of the situation? How does it impact you? How does it impact others? Empathise with, and practice the position of, someone who might resist the change. How could you make this an attractive change for them? Then, when you are prepared, make the case and get feedback on your approach. What would have made you more persuasive and ultimately successful?

*"'I'm sorry, Shelley," Nick began.
"I know you are fed up with hearing this."*

Forgiveness & Permission

A good ScrumMaster will push for permission to remove impediments to team productivity. A great ScrumMaster will be prepared to ask for forgiveness.

Scrum teams will come up against many impediments that require some creative and/or courageous approaches. Perhaps it's saying no to overtime, hosting the retrospective in the pub or maybe it's buying an ad-hoc server from the local computer shop on the corporate credit card because lead times are so high within the internal processes. Great ScrumMasters take the approach that, so long as it is legal, ethical and defensible in the pursuit of quality delivery, if the team need something then it is their job to give it to them.

To help illustrate this point, I want to share the story of Shelley, a new ScrumMaster who was helping her team deal with the very real pain involved with working in a new way while satisfying old requirements.

"I'm sorry, Shelley," Nick began. "I know you are fed up with hearing this but I think we have to talk about the tool again. It's such a pain having to update ScrumLog as well as our board and it's not getting any easier."

Shelley knew that this was going to come up in the retrospective because the team had been getting more and more frustrated about the dual-entry and the clunky nature of the tool.

"There's no need to apologise, Nick," Shelley responded. "I feel your pain. I don't like using it either."

"Why do we need to use it at all? We have everything we need to know on this wall." Nick asked

"I think you are right and I can see how using the tool seems like double-entry, especially when it's not very intuitive, and you have all those fields to complete just to add a task," Shelley replied sympathetically. "Is there anything you do like about the tool?"

"Sure. It does nice, pretty graphs and I can see the state of the wall when I'm working at home or in the other office," Nick admitted.

"And it's nice to have all of the stories backed up electronically for posterity and safekeeping," Suzie suggested.

"OK. So what could I do to help?" Shelley asked.

"Could we trial another tool, say ESB, to see if it's any better? " Nick asked.

"Personally I don't mind what tool you try out. My only issue is that, if you like it, then it's bound to cost money and the company have decided to invest in ScrumLog," Shelley said. She paused for a moment to think about how their product owner Karen might react. "I could have a word with Karen to see if she could find some budget but I can't make any promises."

"Fair enough," said Nick. "So can we have a play with the free versions of a couple of tools this sprint to see if they are any good then?"

"So long as it doesn't affect the velocity too much I'm sure it wouldn't be a problem. I think we should just clear it with Karen, though, to be sure," Shelley said.

After the retrospective, Shelley went to Karen's office and explained that the issue of a less cumbersome tool had come up at the retrospective over the past few sprints. She broached the topic of setting aside some sprint time to research better tool options. While Karen was open to the teams trying out one of the tools this sprint, she cautioned that she did not have any spare budget to pay for the licences after the trial period expired.

Shelley brought the news back to the team: It looked like they were stuck with ScrumLog for the time being at least.

At the next retrospective, the team brought the issue up once again. This time, Shelley said, "OK, I get it. Let's think about what options we have. We can't pay for another tool while we have corporate licences for ScrumLog but there's nothing stopping us from creating our own."

Nick looked quite excited about this idea. "I didn't think of that. It wouldn't take much to knock up a virtual Scrum board in HTML with a little drag and drop interface, some logging and archiving functionality. We don't need anything complicated and I'm pretty sure we can find a chart creation plug-in for the burndown."

"We could probably knock something basic up in the next couple of days during lunch and after-hours," Suzie suggested.

"But isn't there a corporate directive requiring all teams to use the same tool for standardisation purposes?" AJ asked.

Shelley looked at AJ and nodded. "Yes. That is the rule, but let's worry about that if and when that problem comes up. I'm pretty sure I could defend the decision we are taking to those involved. Especially if we see a boost in productivity as a result," she said.

Follow Your Instincts

The first instinct of any good ScrumMaster is to remove the impediment. If the team are coming up with suggestions for how to solve a problem, then good ScrumMasters generally encourage these ideas and help make them happen.

In this story, Shelley is in a difficult position. She really wants to help her team be effective and remove a big impediment to their productivity. It just so happens that this particular impediment is an organisationally sponsored and mandated tool.

Shelley's first step was to help clear the path for the team to trial new tools and to ask the product owner, Karen, for the necessary budget. When that didn't work, Shelley got more creative and started to explore ways she could help the team avoid the use of the company-mandated tool while still fulfilling the company's reporting requirements. Her solution was to ask the team if they would like to create their own.

She shared AJ's concern that there were likely to be issues down the line but she was confident that they were breaking protocol for the right reasons and could justify the team's actions if it became necessary.

Value Principles over Rules

Shelley isn't the first ScrumMaster to bend the rules to help her team, and she won't be the last. I once worked with a company that tried to standardise Scrum all the way down to the sprint length. One of the teams felt strongly that a two-week sprint worked much better than the company-mandated four-week sprint. Initially their ScrumMaster tried to make the case for every team being allowed to pick the Sprint length that was appropriate for their circumstances but the arguments fell on deaf ears.

So, like Shelley, the ScrumMaster decided to work around the existing rules to best serve the team. The only thing stopping the team from going to two-week sprints was the fact that they would have to hold a review, retrospective, and second sprint planning very quietly. The ScrumMaster talked to the team, and they agreed that the benefits of shorter sprints outweighed the risk of working outside guidelines. The team shifted to two-week sprints, but continued to maintain the illusion that they were using four-week sprints. They also agreed to collect some data, so that the ScrumMaster could later make a case—based on empirical evidence—that the team were much more productive when working in shorter sprints.

I know this sounds like I am encouraging insubordination and, to a degree, I suppose I am. The transition to an agile organisation is bound to see a few conflicts arise when the teams who are trying to be agile come up against the less-than-agile processes of the traditional organisation. Sometimes the only way to push change is to be disobedient. However, as I've reminded you a couple of times now, a dead ScrumMaster is a useless ScrumMaster.

Think these things through carefully. You might be surprised how easy it is to make a case for a trial of an alternative process when using Scrum.

The time-boxed nature of sprints and the opportunity to gather data quickly are in your favour.

A Note on Tools

I get asked about tools all the time. My response has always been the same. There are many tools out there aimed at Scrum teams and they are all 100 times better than the tools we had ten years ago. The functionality and the options they have are amazing. The good news, then, is that almost no matter what the team want to do, the latest tools have an option to do it, even when their process changes over time. Unfortunately having all that functionality is also a bad thing because there is a risk that someone will find a reason for using that functionality.

For example, if there is the possibility of having an extra line on the burndown that calculates estimate accuracy then you can be sure that a manager somewhere will be interested in that data. Pretty soon, the tool starts driving the process and becomes a burden on the team rather than enabling them to be effective. This is why almost all of the great Scrum teams that I have seen either use physical tools (cards, stickies etc) or the most minimalistic tool they can find—and it's often one that they have created themselves!

"I know this sounds like I am encouraging insubordination and, to a degree, I suppose I am. Sometimes the only way to push change is to be disobedient."

Some days only two or three team members were at the daily scrum; the rest were busy with other commitments.

Eliminating Distractions

A good ScrumMaster protects the team from distractions. A great ScrumMaster finds the root cause of those distractions and eliminates them.

I believe that teams can cope with a couple of non-dedicated people on the team, even though it is not ideal. In his book, *Succeeding with Agile* [1], Mike Cohn says that organisations should "minimise the number of people required to be on two teams and avoid having anyone on three." If nothing else, having people who are 49 percent or less allocated to a project sends the message that there is something else more important somewhere else and, by definition, *x* percent of your time is being spent on something less important.

In my experience, any organisation that refers to its people as resources and believes they are fungible is going to really struggle with Scrum. While Scrum doesn't mandate that nobody should work on more than one team or project, its values of focus and commitment and its dependence upon teamwork do seem to call for it. I would find it hard to describe the people in the following story as a true team.

The Wizard Sleeves were a team of seven people—Alistair, Dave, Gordon, Margaret, Nicola, Olivier, and Peter—pulled together from various project teams within the department to tackle a piece of work that had been hanging around for about a year. At sprint planning Tony, the Scrum-Master (and also one of the management team in the department), brought along a resource planning table to show how much time each of the team members had available to spend on this project.

Not only was every member of the team assigned to other projects, this was not even the primary project for over half the team. Only Olivier could say that this was his priority one project.

Sprint planning was tough for the team. The resource planner didn't indicate *when* each person was available—was Dave available for the first third of the sprint? The last third? 33 percent of every day? The first third of every week? How was that going to synchronise with the other team members' availability?

The team ended up committing to a lot less than they would have liked to because of the uncertainty, which did not please Tony, but at least they were on their way.

Unfortunately, the sprint didn't go much better than sprint planning. The team never seemed to really be together. Some days only two or three team members were at the daily scrum; the rest were busy with other commitments. The team members asked Tony to deal with an assortment of impediments, most of which revolved around not having access to the teammates they needed when they needed them. While Tony was busy trying to help, the blocked team members would just move on—after all they had plenty to work on, it was just all on other projects! By the time Tony tracked down the necessary teammate or information, the blocked teammate was busy with something else. As a result, the sprint burndown started off badly and got progressively worse, ultimately ending in a failed sprint and a demoralised team.

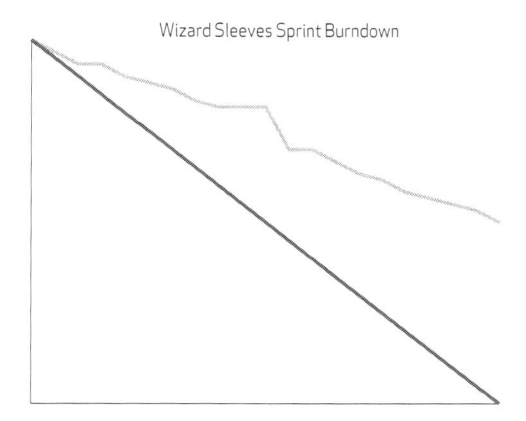

Wizard Sleeves Sprint Burndown

By the end of the sprint, it was clear to Tony that the team needed to find ways to coordinate their available time during the sprint more effectively. He crafted the goal of the retrospective to ask the team:

"How would you ideally organise your availability in this sprint to maximise your ability to deliver?"

Tony led the team through the identification and evaluation of various options for organising themselves including:

- Identifying dependencies and working out mini critical-paths throughout the team
- Putting off their other commitments for one sprint to just focus on the Wizard Sleeves and then go back to their other projects for a few months
- Identifying certain "Wizard Sleeves hours" each day where the team could commit to coming together and working on this project

- Identifying a number of contiguous days where the team could just focus on the Wizard Sleeves' product backlog (e.g. Mondays & Tuesdays)
- Altering the sprint length either up or down to see if that helped

Of all these options, the team thought that having a shorter, focussed sprint just concentrating on the Wizard Sleeves' product backlog would be their preferred choice as this would reduce their context switching.

After the meeting, Tony spoke to the other various product owners and management and managed to secure a trial period. In the trial sprint the team actually delivered more in two weeks than they had in the previous four-week sprint, mainly because of a greater focus. Tony then used the empirical data to make a case to management for a change to how people were assigned to projects and teams.

The Parallel Approach

Let's take a very simplistic model, where one individual has three tasks that are each one-week's worth of work: task A, task B and task C. They decide to take them all on simultaneously. In the first week, they will do a little bit of task A, a little bit of task B and a little bit of task C:

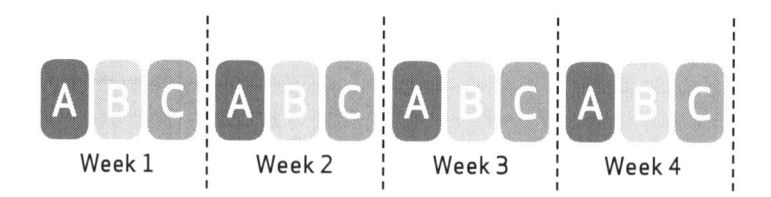

A B C | A B C | A B C | A B C
Week 1 | Week 2 | Week 3 | Week 4

The first thing that you will notice is that, by taking on three one-week tasks concurrently, it will likely take *four weeks* to complete them all. This is because of the cost of context switching. The inefficiencies of context switching are widely known so I won't delve into the science behind it.

Even if we assume that there are no costs of context switching—and that these tasks do actually get completed in three weeks—this would still be a bad way of working compared to the serial approach described below.

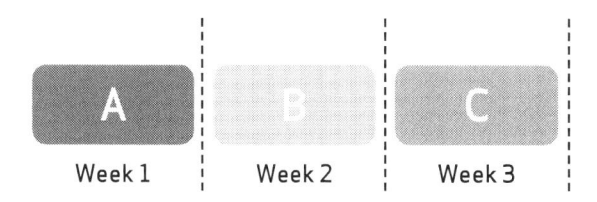

The Serial Approach

In a serial approach, we would work on and finish task A in week one, then work on and finish task B in week two, then focus solely on task C in week three. We finish all three tasks in three weeks, and we have the extra benefit of being able to benefit from finished tasks after weeks one and two.

Though a parallel approach may make us feel like we are making more progress, we are actually in a worse position. In most cases, the reality of context switching means the three tasks will take longer overall. Even if you manage to somehow buck all the science and bring your tasks in with a *zero cost* of context switching, you would still not have anything completed at the end of week one, or the end of week two. The serial approach is simply more efficient.

Responding To Change

The serial approach, besides giving us a shorter time from task start to task completion, has another distinct advantage over a parallel approach: increased adaptability. What if, at the end of week one, a new, really important task comes up—task X—that is conveniently enough a week's worth of effort again? What do we do? Well, if it's really important, we drop what we are working on and start work on it. However, the parallel versus serial approaches give us drastically different results. If we are working on tasks A, B & C concurrently, we have to drop work on all three tasks in order to pick up X (unless we just add X into the mix and now work on four items simultaneously!). However, if we have already finished task A, then we have a clean slate and can pick the most important thing to work on next, which in this case would be task X.

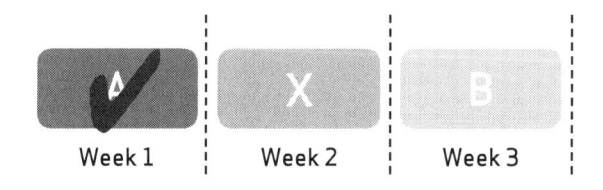

| Week 1 | Week 2 | Week 3 |

Project Realities

Having every team member solely focused on one project is a laudable, if somewhat impossible, aim. Sometimes it will actually make sense for people to be shared across projects, as it would be a complete waste of their time to be entirely focussed on one project if their skills just won't be needed for the whole sprint.

Teams can adopt simple rules to increase their effectiveness, such as, "Everyone on the team must be at least 60 percent allocated to the team" or "No more than four people can be on two projects."

Most organisations fool themselves into believing that having multiple projects on the go at one time will actually increase their productivity—and the happiness—of their people. The truth is, if they actually cut a number of their projects, they would see productivity and happiness rise. I would much rather wait until the ROI of one project falls low enough to allow us to focus on a new one and staff it properly than to work on multiple projects. ScrumMasters should strive for this focus, as it directly affects both team productivity and organisational ROI.

Good ScrumMasters will find ways to help teams make the best of their situations and minimise disturbances, whether that means re-organising the team so that they are able to focus for the sprint or running interference against anyone who is looking to talk to the team about something other than their sprint commitments. Great ScrumMasters do this at first but also tend to dive deep and find the root cause of team distractions, in this case pushing the problem of multi-tasking at a project level back up the management chain rather than making team members cope with it. Making the case for more focussed teams and more focussed individuals is something that will be appreciated by the individuals and teams involved but also, in the medium to long-term, the whole organisation.

*"You already planned it out?"
Xander asked. "Why?"
"Didn't you trust the team?"*

Surviving The Corporate Culture

*A good ScrumMaster helps
a Scrum team survive in an organisation's culture.
A great ScrumMaster helps change the culture
so Scrum teams can thrive.*

There are many ways that an organisation's culture may need to change in order for Scrum teams to thrive. Perhaps your organisation has a culture of micro-management, or a performance management system that encourages individual development and the growth of heroes. Perhaps your organisation is structured in a matrix-style, applying an individualistic approach to resourcing projects, or perhaps there is a historic desire to fix both time and scope on projects.

There are many more examples of corporate cultures that can conflict with Scrum teams. Great ScrumMasters realise that changes in corporate DNA are not going to happen overnight; they will mutate over time given the right conditions and stimuli. Sometimes simply making visible the dysfunction or bottleneck will be sufficient (such as highlighting the causes, consequences and cost of technical debt), sometimes change will require influence, persuasion or lobbying, and other times it will require evidence of a valid alternative path before anyone will listen. Whatever the strategy, great ScrumMasters take a viral approach: slow enough to not get destroyed by the host organisation but quick enough to gather momentum and instigate structural change within the corporate DNA.

The following story is unfortunately all too common and a situation that many ScrumMasters will have to overcome.

The Blockheads team was fairly new to each other and to Scrum. As such, they had little idea of their true velocity. Their new project was fairly complex as well. After four hours of release planning and some intense facilitation by their ScrumMaster Xander, the Blockheads came up with an estimate of six sprints (six months) to complete their first release.

Heleena, Xander's manager, had been observing this new practice of agile planning. After it was over, she pulled Xander to one side.

"Six months? That's ridiculous. We can't afford to take six months to get this release out," she said.

"Well, we do have the option of deploying any time after sprint three, so we could call this two releases really," Xander replied.

"But it's still going to take us six months to get all the functionality finished isn't it?"

"It looks that way with the information we have at the moment, but it could be quicker or it could even be longer," Xander explained. "This plan is just an aggregation of approximations based on little practical evidence of this team working on this type of problem."

"Well, I worked through these requirements with a couple of other managers the other day and we calculated it would take three-to-four months, nearly half the estimate of the team here," Heleena said.

"You already planned it out?" Xander asked. "Why?"

"To give myself a baseline to assess the team's plan. I had no idea what they were going to come up with and wanted to know if it was reasonable."

"In other words you didn't trust the team," Xander inferred.

"It's not that I didn't trust them, it's just that they aren't used to doing this and, well, this idea of the team doing the planning is bound to lead to teams under-committing isn't it?" Heleena tried to explain.

"So what are you going to do with this information?" Xander asked.

"Well, I'm hoping you can encourage them to revisit the plan to see if they can find a way to bring the timescales down," Heleena finished.

All Plans Are Wrong

Xander is in a difficult situation here. This team is new and so the plan is very likely going to be wrong. All plans are arguably wrong anyway because, as soon as they are made, the information used to make them is immediately out of date. This is magnified when a team is new and the problem is complex.

Team empowerment is a key part of Scrum; giving the team the space to establish their capability is a massive contributor to that. In practice, it often takes teams about three or four sprints to establish a steady, predictable velocity, before which time they tend to fluctuate between over-promising and over-delivering. In the future you are also likely to see the velocity of the team accelerate further as the team get more familiar with each other and optimise their processes.

While the team is figuring things out, it might be worth considering shorter sprints to get some empirical data about team velocity earlier. This will help establish trust with management, who might be feeling a bit afraid of whether "this whole agile thing" will even work. That being said, shorter sprints should be weighed up against the extra overhead and strain on a team. For more on sprint lengths see the chapter "How Long Is a Piece Of String?".

One of the big benefits of Scrum is that the product owner has the opportunity to re-evaluate the company's gamble on the project every sprint. If, after one sprint, the release plan has expanded to nine sprints, chances are the project will be stopped or a more experienced team chosen, because the projected costs will be too high with the current team. However, if the team velocity is higher than predicted and the release plan shrinks to five sprints, the product owner will feel much better about the chances of success.

Attempting to encourage, pressure or bribe the team into reducing the release plan will almost certainly lead to the team either consciously or sub-consciously cutting quality and introducing technical debt.

Trust and Principles

Although establishing release plans with any new team is difficult, the more subtle problem in this situation is the lack of trust of the team. If the team were to find out that their plan would only count if it met the expectations of the product owner or management, then their buy-in to the process and the project would undoubtedly diminish. They would then have little chance of achieving the productivity and creativity benefits offered by a self-managing Scrum team.

To quote former American politician Henry Stimson: "The only way to make a man trustworthy is to trust him."

While we must sometimes make short-term compromises for long-term gains, great ScrumMasters know when it is imperative to take a stand on principle for the sake of the long-term agility, performance and integrity of the organisation. They might educate stakeholders and management about the benefits of self-management and the general advantages of team-buy in. They might also help calculate and visually represent the costs of the technical debt that will likely result from pressuring the team into meeting a fixed scope by an imposed deadline.

That being said, while advocating for their teams, ScrumMasters must be careful about how they approach the situation. It's critical that any arguments be presented calmly and factually. Explaining the danger of undermining the team's autonomy and self-management and emphasising the cost of poor quality will go a long way toward helping management understand the importance of trusting the team.

Organisations that compromise the integrity of their products—and working at an unrealistic or unsustainable pace is the quickest way to do this—will soon accumulate technical debt that slows down their performance. Once this happens, there is even greater pressure on estimated project timescales, which only exacerbates the problem. It is a very slippery slope. Great ScrumMasters halt that slide quickly but tactfully.

*"I don't get it, Jas.
Scrum is supposed to be all about self-management,
and I was told on the training course that people would love
the autonomy that Scrum would give them."*

An ORGANIC culture

A good ScrumMaster helps a team become agile.
A great ScrumMaster helps a team become coherent.

"This sprint has been, as Forrest Gump would say, just like a box of chocolates," said Quinn, one of the developers in the Buccaneers team at their end of sprint retrospective.

"Tell me more," said Vic, the ScrumMaster.

"Well everything in the box (or in our case the sprint) looks the same on the outside but everyone seems to be eating something different," explained Quinn.

"Yeah, and sometimes you bite into something expecting it to be a chewy caramel but it turns out to be a raisin! Eurgh!" added Sutton, another Buccaneers developer.

"And that would translate to the real world how exactly?" asked Vic, smiling.

"You know, that you go to work on one thing but it turns out to be something else or we get hijacked by something more important," explained Sutton.

"We've been supposed to be trying this agile way of doing things but I'm not sure it's working," said Quinn. "Take our own product owner, for instance. Gray seems much more interested in ensuring the existing product is working well, than helping us determine what needs to happen to get the new product out the door. It seems as though the existing product always takes priority, and we're not able to make much progress as a result."

"Gray has definitely been spending a lot of time with customers on bugs and change requests recently," conceded Vic, "but we have the framework to deal with that. We just need to stick to the process and not allow ourselves to get distracted."

"With all due respect, Vic, I don't think that's enough. Nobody seems to really care about what we're doing and I think we need to escalate it. And when I say we...I of course mean you," said Quinn, smiling mischievously.

"I'm not sure anyone will listen to someone who only went on their Scrum training four weeks ago. Personally I think being tighter on the sprint goal, definition of ready and definition of done like we talked about earlier will be enough to make things better but if you really think it's worth escalating then I'll see what I can do," said Vic.

Later that day Vic mentioned to Gray what the team had said. They agreed to keep a keener eye on things over the next sprint. Things didn't get any better and, despite a public statement from Ali, the COO, that "being agile is really important to the company's future," the number of misunderstandings seemed to get worse. The developers seemed to have given up on reaching consensus on things and, instead, focussed on their own pieces of work, effectively pulling in different directions.

Dreading the next retrospective, Vic reached out to Jas, a recently hired ScrumMaster who was a lot more experienced for some help.

"I don't get it, Jas. Scrum is supposed to be all about self-management, and I was told on the training course that people would love the autonomy that Scrum would give them. The trainer said that, when given the opportunity, people will naturally gravitate towards self-management because of the sense of purpose that a common goal will give them," Vic said.

"Well that certainly can happen," replied Jas, "but my experience tells me that there's a lot more to self-management than just putting a team together and telling them to go for it. The best teams that I've seen have all made a conscious effort to understand each other's value systems and work out some explicit expectations of one another, and then their collective expectations with others such as the Product Owner and leadership in general within the organisation."

"That sounds sensible but scary. I wouldn't even know where to start with all of that," said Vic.

"It's honestly not as scary as it sounds. I've got an activity you could run with them if you like," said Jas, and then proceeded to explain how Vic could go about it.

At the team's daily scrum, Vic said to the team, "I know we're all busy but for our retrospective this sprint, I would like us all to do a little bit of preparation. I've been doing a bit of research on the frustrations you've all mentioned and I think I've got something we can do that will help us."

"I want you all to think of some specific examples of things that have not gone well since we started work on the new product and working with Scrum. I want you to think of them as if they were stories and capture them on sticky notes with a title, a brief description of what happened and, if possible, a moral of the story."

"I want you to do the same for examples of when things went well. 3 or 4 stories each would be perfect. That's it. I'm actually really excited about it," said Vic.

At the team's retrospective, everyone turned up with their stories on sticky notes. They also noticed a new person in the room.

"Hi everyone, this is Jas, who joined about a month ago but has worked as a ScrumMaster in four different companies over the last twelve years. I reached out for a bit of advice and it was so great to have someone with a bit more experience than me. It was Jas who suggested this technique, which sounded great to me. I don't know enough about it to be able to facilitate it well so Jas has agreed to step in and facilitate it for us if that's OK with you all."

Everyone in the team agreed and Jas thanked them for their acceptance.

"Before we get to your sticky notes, I'd like to just briefly talk through a number of different leadership archetypes that are pretty common in most organisations. The one thing I want to stress right now is that none of them are essentially good or bad, so try and think of them as objectively as possible if you can."

Jas then proceeded to explain the following archetypes.

THE EXPERT
In this archetype, the leader is in position because of the amount of knowledge, experience and expertise they have. Put simply, they know more than anyone else about what needs to be done, why it needs to be done and how it needs to be done. Because of this, they are the perfect person to tell others what needs to be done and how.

THE CO-ORDINATOR
Here the leader is responsible for the group working together effectively. They retain most of the responsibility for making decisions, resolving conflict and effective communication but they will encourage some participation.

THE PEER
When the leader adopts the peer archetype they position themselves as an equal member of the group so decision making is naturally more shared and there is a lot more peer to peer feedback rather than going through the leader. The rest of the group then take on more responsibility for how things are done and for the results they produce.

THE COACH
When the leader is a coach, they are effectively positioning themselves outside of the team and the team themselves are solely responsible for organising themselves, making decisions, co-ordinating each other and achieving results. The leader is now focusing on setting the strategic direction and helping the team and the individuals within it grow through reflection, feedback and coaching.

THE STRATEGIST
The team are now in a position to influence strategy and expand their scope of self-management outside of their own boundaries. The leader is encouraging this and acts as a conduit, maintaining the connection between the organisational strategy and the (possibly multiple) team's feedback.

After explaining the archetypes to the team, Jas invited them to read out their stories to the group before placing their sticky notes on to the archetype that they felt was in play in their stories. After everyone had gone, Jas asked the group what they noticed.

"Well the first thing I noticed was how we had different interpretations of what success and failure were, even though the stories themselves were quite similar," said Quinn.

"Yeah, me too," added Gray. "And it's interesting how some people felt that they needed more guidance from me while others felt I was micro-managing sometimes. I guess I don't understand what kind of archetype is right for me."

"The way I understood it is that there isn't necessarily one right archetype for you but to understand what the particular story requires of you at that point. Is that right, Jas?" asked Vic.

"Spot on, Vic. It's all about coherence. I've been in organisations where leadership has told people to self-organise but then continued to constrain them to the point where they had no agency. I've been in other organisations where the team has been crying out for autonomy but the leadership continue to tell them what to do. And I've been in other organisations where the leadership has effectively told them to just get on with things because they are now self-managing. All of those situations have led to what we call motivational debt because it wasn't what the team was expecting or felt ready for," Jas explained.

"I like that term: motivational debt!" said Sutton.

"If you had to pick one of these archetypes to base your work together on which would you pick?" asked Jas.

Everyone thought before all agreeing on the peer archetype but with a general desire to move more towards a coach archetype over time.

"So my challenge to you would be to work out amongst yourselves what you need from one another in order for your work to be successful if this is your desired current archetype," said Jas.

The team discussed how important it is to act as peers, calling each other out, making decisions together and holding each other accountable to their shared goal. Other factors such as being braver around decision-making and resolving conflict rather than avoiding it were called out as well. Everyone left the retrospective confident that they had a new shared understanding of where they are and perhaps where they might be heading over time.

ORGANIC agility™

These archetypes are taken from the ORGANIC Leadership model which is part of ORGANIC agility [2], an approach at helping organisations develop greater resilience in the face of ever-increasing volatility, uncertainty, complexity and ambiguity (VUCA) in their domain or industry. In such an environment, it is important to be coherent in your leadership approach and to aim for a culture that is coherent with the demands placed on the organisation and team.

ORGANIC is both an acronym and a metaphor. Traditionally organisations are built upon a mechanical metaphor, where a more efficient processing of inputs leads to greater output. These organisations are built for robustness so they can withstand the threats we know about. This metaphor, and structure, works in an environment of stability, predictability and repeatability.

When we are in a more VUCA type environment, we need a more ORGANIC approach, a structure that rapidly evolves to meet the unknown threats and can reform itself to remain resilient.

To this end, the acronym stands for:

ORGANISATIONAL
RESILIENCE *(by)*
GROWING
AUTONOMY *(and)*
NURTURING *(an)*
INTERDEPENDENT
CULTURE

In a fast-paced and complex environment, where we don't have the time for a decision to be escalated to the leader and back down again and, indeed, even if we did things are so complex that it is unlikely that this person has all the answers, we need greater autonomy. While autonomy has huge advantages, there is one big downside: if all teams have autonomy, we lack standardisation.

Scaling Scrum has been a big topic ever since Scrum was first taken on inside large organisations. Various attempts have been made at creating frameworks to standardise the practices of an agile team. Great Scrum-Masters realise that being agile isn't the goal, but rather remaining continually coherent in an ever-changing world is the key to sustainability and relevance.

So an ORGANIC culture attempts to balance both of these conflicting demands by helping those within the organisation become coherent not around actions but rather beliefs and expectations.

Coherence

Coherence is a fractal concept. It is just as important for the members of a team to be on the same page about how they are working and why, as it is for the culture of the organisation to be appropriate for the domain they are operating within. An important first step here is to visualise where we currently are and then collectively evaluate how coherent that feels. Using stories as reference points is a really good way of doing that because ultimately, stories about how we do things and why are what makes up the culture of a team and an organisation.

A mistake that I have seen many organisations make, albeit an honest one, is to treat their journey as an "agile transformation." It's not a transformation because that implies there is an end state where we have transformed. This is unrealistic in such a fast-changing environment. It is more helpful to think of it as an evolutionary journey. In this evolutionary journey (or continuous transition) it is better to objectively identify and leverage the existing state of things today, rather than depicting an ideal future state that might be unrealistic.

In the story, Jas helped Vic and the team identify how they were working currently, so they could think about the next step to get them closer to their desired future culture. Great ScrumMasters meet every individual where they are, with a positive interpretation of their intent (everyone is trying to be successful) and then help the team see how well they are aligned (or how coherent they are) with one another. Then, they can try something different to help them work towards their next version of themselves, redefining their relationships and expectations as they go.

Have BELIEF

We have talked a lot about the characteristics of great ScrumMasters. Getting RE-TRAINED is hard work; it is a personal journey and it takes a unique individual to do this. You can't do this without what I call BELIEF. This encompasses what I consider the key areas of growth for truly great ScrumMasters.

BELIEVE

A good ScrumMaster will use Scrum to help bring out the best in everyone.
A great ScrumMaster will use Scrum to create a "new best" for everyone.

Believing in the potential of the team first of all requires belief in yourself. This is not an easy task. And yet it is vital. Great ScrumMasters have a positive view of human nature and the capacity for both themselves and others to do great things.

The Rosenthal-Jacobson study (1968) showed the existence of what has become known as the Pygmalion Effect [1]. In the study, teachers were told that the results of tests showed (a randomly selected) 20 percent of their class could be expected to be "spurters" that year and do better than expected in comparison to their classmates. Despite these children being selected at random, the mere fact that the teachers expected them to do better led to a statistically significant gain in IQ. What could your team be capable of if you genuinely believed in your potential as well as theirs?

ENQUIRE

A good ScrumMaster asks to understand.
A great ScrumMaster asks so the team can understand.

You have to believe that you have more to learn from the team than you have to tell the team. All great ScrumMasters enquire rather than assume; they resist the temptation to provide answers for the team. Great ScrumMasters are able to let go of the view that they have the answer to the team's problem. Instead they believe that either the individual in question, or the team in general, already knows the answer to their own dilemma (or at least can work it out). They remove their egos and enquire genuinely.

Additionally, we all have a natural curiosity; it is all too easy to ask questions to indulge that side of ourselves. The great ScrumMasters enquire not to gain information for themselves but rather to help provide information and clarity for the team.

LISTEN

A good ScrumMaster will listen carefully to what is said.
A great ScrumMaster will also listen carefully to what is not said.

People have a tendency to be formulating their response while someone is speaking. They are not truly listening. Great ScrumMasters work hard on active listening. They practice withholding their response. They build on their practice of enquiry by listening for the real meaning behind the words. People know when you are listening actively or simply hearing the words. Their behaviour will change simply by knowing that you are genuinely interested in what they have to say. If you listen hard enough, you can even pick up on what they don't, or won't, say as well.

And through this hard work of listening, great ScrumMasters bring more information forward for the team. Listening and reflecting helps the team bring new insights to light. Bringing these insights forward before bringing your own is hard. But this is what is required to be great.

ILLUMINATE

A good ScrumMaster will guide
the team through the inevitable stages of development.
A great ScrumMaster holds the mirror up to the team and
the wider organisation so they can reflect and grow.

The great ScrumMasters are all willing and able to play back what they are hearing, offering their observations to the team for them to consider and reflect upon. As great ScrumMasters are carefully enquiring and listening to exactly what is said (and what is not), they illuminate potential interpretations and new insights. They also monitor behaviours for patterns, inconsistencies and destructive habits or tendencies—not to judge but to hold the mirror up so the team can reflect and then inspect and adapt.

To do this means that the great ScrumMaster must illuminate and reflect on their own behaviours and inconsistencies first. They are prepared to face their weaknesses and elevate their strengths through this illumination.

ENCOURAGE

A good ScrumMaster coaches the team to success.
A great ScrumMaster also allows room for failure

There is no constant. Change is the only constant. If you aren't moving forward, then you're moving backward. You've heard all the catchphrases, and many of them are true. Today, organisations need to be constantly adapting; and teams need to be constantly adapting as well. Scrum has built-in opportunities to improve, so encourage your team in whatever way you can to take advantage of them. Even if it's just a small change, or a small experiment, never let a sprint go by without something new being attempted. This builds habit and muscle memory.

Reducing the cost, the fear and the risk of trying something new is key, so make it fun and make it OK to fail. Remember, failure is OK as long as we fail quickly, we fail cheaply and we don't fail the same way twice.

Great ScrumMasters not only act as cheerleaders for the team but also need to provide this service to themselves. It is a lonely job at times and, to encourage others, great ScrumMasters must work on their own inner strengths.

FACILITATE

A good ScrumMaster helps the team find ways to optimise their process. A great ScrumMaster guides the team past the need for process (and a ScrumMaster).

Facilitation is the underpinning skill and behaviour of all great Scrum-Masters. At all times, great ScrumMasters are of service to the goals of the team, the product owner and the organisation. And, if those goals conflict, they think of the long-term implications and the messages any compromise will send. They facilitate relationships both within the team and also between the team and those outside the team. They facilitate the Scrum process and the evolution of the process. They facilitate the integration of the Scrum team into the wider organisation and the changing of that organisation to actively support Scrum.

Great ScrumMasters work relentlessly on themselves in order to become excellent facilitators. They introspect, they retrospect, they seek insights from others about their work. And they pair with other ScrumMasters in order to continue their growth. However, great ScrumMasters ultimately know that none of this is about themselves. This does not mean that they are not ambitious—far from it. However their ambition is for the success of others.

Their own personal success is judged by how well they facilitate others to do their jobs, by how much they are not noticed or relied upon, and by how quickly and effectively they can step away from the team they have helped create.

Eventually, you may even find yourself facilitating your team away from Scrum; once they have their hairy shoes (see Chapter "Above All, Empower the Team" for an explanation of Shu Ha Ri). Great ScrumMasters understand this can be a good thing, given that the team is ready and the time is right, and could be the ultimate sign of a job well done.

Appendices

ScrumMaster Is a Full Time Role

One of the most common questions I get asked is, "So do you really expect someone to just be a ScrumMaster?" Most people find it hard to believe that this role will take up their whole day, five days a week. They believe that, because the team is self-managing and the product owner is more involved, all the ScrumMaster needs to do is run the meetings.

Many organisations try to use part-time ScrumMasters. This has the dual benefit of saving money and keeping their most talented employees in their existing roles. What it also does, however, is prevent these organisations from true success with Scrum, which costs them money and squanders potential over the long term.

Let's look at three common examples of the part-time ScrumMaster, all of which introduce a conflict of interests to some degree, and examine the pros and cons of each.

The ScrumMaster & Product Owner Combination

Let's start with the easiest example—the ScrumMaster/product owner. My advice here is quite simple—don't do it! The roles are separate for a reason. The product owner is responsible for ensuring that we are doing the right stuff in order to maximise the return on investment of the project or product. The team is responsible for doing the stuff right; to deliver value as quickly as possible while maintaining high quality. The ScrumMaster is responsible for the integrity of the team and the process itself. The tension between the ScrumMaster's attention to the process and the product owner's focus on the product fosters a yin-yang balance and mutually beneficial interdependence.

Merging the ScrumMaster and product owner roles removes the balance and thus the neutrality of the role. There will no longer be any neutral facilitation, no protection of the team or the process. There will always be at least a suspicion of an ulterior motive to every conversation and no sense of safety for the team to grow and experiment. I have never seen these two roles combined successfully

The ScrumMaster & Team Member Combination

By far the most common example of the part-time ScrumMaster is when a team member takes on the extra role of ScrumMaster. This usually happens either because an organisation doesn't yet believe that a full-time ScrumMaster is necessary or, as is more often the case, is unwilling to pay for a full-time ScrumMaster.

Having a ScrumMaster/Team Member (I will refer to this dual role as SM/TM going forward) does have a few advantages. If the ScrumMaster also has developer responsibilities, then that person likely can already speak the same language and can empathise with the other developers straight away. The other developers are more likely to be open and transparent with the SM/TM and it's a lot easier for the SM/TM to read between the lines of what's going on in the team.

Unfortunately, in practice, the dual role of SM/TM compromises both the development efforts of the individual and the effectiveness of the ScrumMaster role, usually leading to lower team velocity, so I strongly discourage it.

One of the first, and biggest issues with a SM/TM shows up in planning. A team member who is not totally committed (which is effectively what a SM/TM becomes) poses a problem for the team: Just how much time should be set aside for development work this sprint, and how much time for ScrumMaster tasks? Nobody knows.

Product backlog items are discrete work items that are nonetheless difficult to estimate. What you will need to do as a ScrumMaster this sprint, on the other hand, is impossible to predict much less account for in terms of time. ScrumMasters are often interrupted or redirected to team issues rather than product backlog items. It's hard, therefore, to trust a SM/TM with high-risk or high-priority items.

Many teams solve this problem by having the SM/TM focus more on the lower risk items, letting the full-time team members tackle the higher risk and higher priority items. This mitigates risk but also means that sometimes the best person isn't working on the right task.

The two most common strategies teams use to help alleviate these problems are to assume the ScrumMaster role will occupy 100 percent of the time or to assign the ScrumMaster role an arbitrary percentage of time.

Assume ScrumMaster Will Have No Time To Develop

In this scenario, the team plan their capacity assuming the SM/TM is not going to contribute toward any product backlog items. If the SM/TM does have time to help with a task or two, the team treats it as a bonus. This is the simplest, cleanest and, arguably, the best way to deal with this dual role when it comes to planning capacity. The team know what they are planning for and are more likely to meet their commitments because of the extra certainty (and the potential bonus contribution of the Scrum-Master). The team don't have to worry about the ScrumMaster signing up for important development tasks and not being able to finish them. SM/TMs, however, tend to miss having development work and worry that their development skills will become rusty. This can, over time, cause a significant amount of resentment in the SM/TM.

You could argue, and I have many times, that if you are planning around this person being a ScrumMaster 100 percent of the time, wouldn't it be better to make it formal and build it into the budget? Either actually make this person a full-time ScrumMaster and backfill with another team member or hire another full-time ScrumMaster and let this person concentrate on being a great developer.

Split The Role on an Arbitrary Basis (Usually 50:50)

In this scenario, we just make a guess about how the SM/TM will split the responsibilities of the dual-role. The SM/TM will typically not sign up to any of the bigger, riskier items on the sprint backlog because there is a much greater chance of being dragged off to be a ScrumMaster. It's much more sensible for them to pick up the smaller, simpler tasks, leaving the rest of the team to carry the larger load.

While many teams will gravitate towards this strategy in order for the developer to keep their hand in, the SM/TMs still aren't working on important or interesting development work, and cannot fully commit to the ScrumMaster role either. As such, resentment is likely to develop in this scenario as well.

A very common outcome in this scenario is that, towards the end of the sprint, the SM/TM becomes overloaded and has to choose between development tasks and ScrumMaster tasks. When this happens, the SM/TM will fail at one of the dual roles, which is both demotivating and unfair.

Authority Issues

There is another subtle issue with this dual-role, which is that the SM/TM is attributed a perceived level of authority slightly greater than everyone else in the team, which harms self-management and team harmony

One option to help with this issue is for teams to rotate the role, so that each developer takes on the dual-role for a sprint at a time. This would remove the implied hierarchical challenges and mitigate the impacts on technical passion. It would also give every member of the team an opportunity to get some experience in removing impediments and serving the team, almost increasing the self-management capabilities of each team member in turn.

However, you are almost certain to have someone in the team who is either unsuitable for this role, or not happy about taking it on and therefore are almost guaranteed to have at least one sprint where the team struggles. Also, a big part of being an effective ScrumMaster is the networking within the organisation: knowing who to speak to and where to go when a certain problem comes up. By only giving each person one sprint to play the role, nobody is going to get the opportunity to build up their network and get their teeth into the role.

Almost without fail, the common denominator in all of the teams who have this dual-role is the loss of the ScrumMaster as an organisational change agent.

The best SM/TMs do manage to keep things ticking over within the team while adding some value on the development side of things. But the external focus of the ScrumMaster role is almost always neglected and this does keep teams – and their organisations - from reaching their potential. Eventually teams hit a plateau and the organisation fails to move forward into the promised land that was talked about when first setting off on the Scrum journey.

Being a ScrumMaster for More than One Team

The third way in which organisations try to employ part-time Scrum-Masters is by dividing one ScrumMaster across several teams. If you focus purely on the basic mechanics of Scrum then you can possibly get away with being a ScrumMaster for more than one team but the more subtle aspects of the role are usually lost when one person tries to take on too much. The people-skills required to be an effective ScrumMaster take up a lot of time. Developing a self-managing team and building the relationships both within the team and between the team and others (such as the product owner, the stakeholders and management) is not an easy thing.

People often argue that focussing on one role for two teams is typically easier, less conflicting and more productive than focussing on two roles for one team. People in this position tell me how it can be beneficial to see a bigger picture outside the scope of a single Scrum team; they can share learning across teams easily and, quite often, resolve impediments that affect multiple teams more efficiently (the old adage of killing two birds with one stone). I have also seen people in this role have greater organisational influence when it comes to removing impediments as they can make the case on behalf of more than one team, thus making it appear to be a bigger impediment than if it was just coming from one team. These benefits are usually increased if the teams are working on a common project as the overlap is significantly greater and the bigger picture is the same piece of art. However, these potential benefits must be weighed against an added difficulty of synchronicity.

Teams on the same project typically synchronise their sprints— it typically makes sense to have one integrated delivery rather than staggered bits of delivery—this means sprint planning and sprint retrospectives happen at the same time. This requires the ScrumMaster to be in two places at once, which is a challenge at best. There will regularly be times during the sprint where both teams need the ScrumMaster as well and, although some things are easier to organise (for example it's not too difficult for team 1 to have their daily scrum at 9:00 and team 2 to have their daily scrum at 9:15) there will be other ad-hoc calls for the ScrumMaster's attention and it will be difficult to have to choose which team to help first.

When I ask people in this situation how they make that decision, they generally tell me "whichever team has the greatest need." They sensibly prioritise based on criticality. However, anyone who has children will tell you that reacting to the one who shouts the loudest will often just lead to increased volume all around and the general escalation of undesired behaviour as each child competes for attention. The most likely outcome here is that, even with the best of intentions, the ScrumMaster will let both teams down, putting both teams at risk of non-delivery and sub-optimisation.

Whenever Possible, Push for a Full-Time Role

Ironically, if you start off as a full-time ScrumMaster, there is a significantly higher likelihood that you could end up as an effective part-time ScrumMaster for multiple teams, as your team will develop their "hairy shoes" much more quickly and be more self-sustaining.

As a bit of parting advice, consider the message that an organisation sends by not supporting the team with the ScrumMaster that Scrum requires.

This is a fundamentally important and full-time role. It isn't really a question of whether the organisation can afford a full-time ScrumMaster but rather whether they can afford *not* to have one. Although the options above are all valid ways of coping with the issue, a better solution would be to look at the issue itself—very much what a ScrumMaster is there to do.

"Ironically, if you start off as a full-time ScrumMaster, there is a significantly higher likelihood that you could end up as an effective part-time ScrumMaster for multiple teams."

Index

5 Whys 47
100 uses 113

A

Acceptance Criteria 75, 159, 171
Accountability 32, 51, 53, 65, 125, 301
Adkins, Lyssa 203, 245
Agile Manifesto 9, 18, 74, 76, 102, 221, 239
Agile Transformation 303
AID Model of Feedback 56
Archetypes 298-301
Art of the Possible 90, 112, 174
Autonomy 62, 131, 174, 192, 293, 297, 300, 302
Awesomeness Backlog 208-210, 221

B

Battle Mapping 61
Boeing 125
Boorstin, Daniel J. 111
Brown, Tim 146
Bulls, Chicago 38
Bullshit Bingo 120
Burndown, Sprint 93-95, 129, 147-148, 195, 198-199, 282
Burnup Graph 186-187, 197
Burnup, Release 186
Burnup, Sprint 187

C

Ceccarelli, Molood 239
Change agent, ScrumMaster as 32
Cheer-leader, ScrumMaster as 308
Cialdini, Robert 51
Coaching 12-13, 26, 38, 56, 93
Coherence 300, 303
Cohn, Mike 9, 14, 281
Collaboration 10, 44-45, 60, 74, 96, 208, 217, 242, 245-247, 255
Collins, Jim 27
Confessions 97
Continuous Positive Regard 237, 266
Core Protocols, The 57

Coronavirus 21, 236
Covey, Stephen 242
Creativity 39, 60, 102, 146, 177, 182, 185, 190, 255, 293
Cross-functional 12, 47, 145-146, 157, 163, 245-246
Culture 21, 26, 55, 57, 107, 142, 245, 266, 289, 295, 301-303

D

Daily Scrum 44-46, 49, 65-66, 68, 93-94, 96-97, 105-107, 115, 117, 119-121, 130, 133-134, 147, 165, 196, 198, 206, 213-214, 242, 248, 252, 255, 282, 317
Derby, Esther 12, 14, 135, 151, 262
Devin, Lee 125
Dickinson, Jean 31
Done, Definition of 152, 157, 163, 252, 296
Donuts 49, 166
Drive 191

E

Elect the ScrumMaster 32
Elephant in the Room 108, 130
Emerson, Ralph Waldo 173
Empathy 242
Empirical 90, 168, 170, 277, 284, 292
Estimation 10, 56, 170, 220, 278, 290-291, 313

F

Facilitation 26, 32, 38, 48, 52, 60, 76, 90, 106, 133, 165, 224, 245, 290, 308, 309, 312
Fist of Five 101

G

Galbraith, J. K. 260
Goddard, Paul 14, 40, 120
Greaves, Karen 180
Greenleaf, Robert K. 26-27, 38
Greg Dollars 186-188, 190
Growing Agile 180
GROW model 263

H

Hook, as Retrospective Tool 136-137
Humility 33

I

IDEO 146
Improv 182, 246-248, 255
Improv Games: Delight 182
Improv Games: First Letter, Last Letter 248
Improv Games: One-Word Storytelling 247, 255
Improv Games: Three-headed Expert 247
Influence 96, 205, 216, 289, 316
Inspiring 13, 28, 143, 173, 185, 191
Integrity 13, 28, 33, 171, 223, 293, 312
Introvert 234, 238
Intuition 138, 247

J

Jackson, Phil 38
Jacobs, Dan 216
Journaling 86

K

Kanban 151
Karate Kid, The 40
King and I, The 189

L

Lady Gaga Sprint, The 191
Laing, Sam 180
Lakers, L.A. 38
Landsberg, Max 56
Larsen, Diana 135
Leadership Archetypes 298-301
Ledru-Rollin, Alexandre 17
Lego 15, 182
Lemonade, Making From Lemons 112
Lencioni, Patrick 43

323

Level 5 Leaders 27
Listening 138, 242-243, 248-249, 306-307
Lotto Factor 146

M

Mama Cass 141
Marshmallow Challenge 143
Matilda 269
McPhee, Nanny 40-41
Micro-Management 198, 289
Millar, Margaret 241
Mirror, ScrumMaster as 27, 129, 307
Modelling Clay 182
Motivation 186, 191-193, 220
Motivational debt 300
MRI 34
Music Conductor, ScrumMaster as 25

N

Nelson Mandela Sprint, The 191
Nokia Test 220-221

O

ORGANIC 21, 295, 301-302
Organisational politics 266-267
Oxygen Mask 85

P

Pairing 67-68, 80, 151, 246
Pandemic 21, 236, 238
Paperclip Challenge 113
Parent, ScrumMaster as 25
Paris Hilton Sprint, The 191
Penny Game 143
Perfection Game, The 57
Performance Management 215-216, 289
Pink, Dan 191

Politician, ScrumMaster as 266
Possible, Art of the 90, 112, 174
Powerful Questions 69, 126-127
Prioritisation 74, 170, 186-191, 206-207, 209, 223-224, 282, 313, 317
Product Backlog 68, 74-75, 101, 147, 149, 152, 158-159, 163, 167-168, 170, 185-191, 207, 220, 284, 313
Project Manager 67
Psychological Safety 237, 238
Purpose 191-192, 198, 248, 297
Push ups 49

R

RAMEN Model 263
Release Plan 168, 171, 290, 292
Remember The Future 137
Remote First 238
Resilience 90, 301, 302
Retrospective 10, 38-39, 44-46, 49, 72-73, 94, 96-97, 100, 123-125, 127, 129, 133-139, 148, 158, 161, 171, 182, 187, 196, 208, 210, 215, 246, 254, 273-275, 277, 283, 295-298, 301, 317
Reward Policies 174, 215
Rock, David 34
Rule of Seven 125

S

Safety, Creating a Sense of 43, 96, 312
Satir, Virginia 201
Schwaber, Ken 89, 142
Screen Fatigue 239
ScrumMaster Circles 113
ScrumMaster Exchange 113
Scrummerfall 160, 163
Self-Managing 17, 18, 38, 47, 108, 195, 208, 245, 293, 311, 316
Self-Talk 81
Servant-Leader 12, 17, 25-27, 32, 35, 38, 82, 90, 142, 213, 223
Seven, rule of 125
Sheepdog, ScrumMaster as 25
Sheriff Badge 152

Shu-Ha-Ri 40-41, 199, 219, 309
Silence 46, 106-108, 148
Southwest Airlines 177, 179
SPEED Coaching 261, 263
Spike 207-208
Sprint Burndown 93-95, 129, 147-148, 195-196, 198-199, 282
Sprint Burnup 197
Sprint Goal 94-95, 135-136, 185, 190-193, 224
Sprint Length 99-100, 102-103, 277, 284
Sprint Limerick 137
Sprint Metaphors 191-192
Sprint Moral 135-137
Sprint Plan 44, 51, 74, 159, 182, 185, 187-188, 195, 206-208, 210, 214, 277, 282, 317
Sprint Review 39, 71, 73-74, 135, 162, 165-171, 175, 186
Stakeholders 75, 97, 165, 167-169, 171, 191, 293, 316
Story Pints 197-198
Supervision 86
Sutherland, Jeff 149

T

Tabaka, Jean 14, 96
TAO of Coaching 56
Team Norms 48-49, 68
Technical Debt 188, 191, 289, 292-293
TED Talks 143, 191
Test Driven Development 160
Testing, as Whole Team Responsibility 145-163, 220
Tom Sawyer Effect 180
Tools 93, 174, 275-276, 278
Truman, Harry 59

U

Unsustainable pace 84, 293
User Manual 231, 233, 235, 237
User Stories 75, 101, 167, 191, 207, 220

V

Velocity 39, 96, 103, 170, 185, 187, 275, 290-292, 313
Vision 245
VUCA 301

W

Waterfall 39, 149, 160, 168, 220
Weather forecast 10, 197, 198
White Knight Syndrome 62, 82, 84
Withdrawal 85

References

Introduction

[1] http://agilemanifesto.org/
[2] https://www.greenleaf.org/what-is-servant-leadership/
[3] Good to Great: Why Some Companies Make the Leap… and Others Don't, Collins, J., 2001, Random House

RETRAINED

[1] http://www.oxfordleadership.com/journal/vol1_issue1/rock.pdf

Respected

[1] http://www.imdb.com/title/tt0396752/quotes
[2] The Five Dysfunctions of a Team: a Leadership Fable, Lencioni, P., 2002, Jossey Bass
[3] http://en.wikipedia.org/wiki/5_Whys
[4] http://en.wikipedia.org/wiki/tuckman's_stages_of_group_development
[5] Influence: Science and Practice, Cialdini, R. B., 2001, Pearson Publishing
[6] https://www.inspectandadapt.com/product/decide-cards-tm
[7] http://en.wikipedia.org/wiki/tuckman's_stages_of_group_development
[8] TAO of Coaching: Boost Your effectiveness at Work by Inspiring and Developing Those Around You, Landsberg, M., 2003, Profile Books
[9] http://www.mccarthyshow.com/online/

Enabling

[1] https://www.thefreedictionary.com/enabling
[2] https://www.youtube.com/watch?v=B_WfnnNUC6o
[3] https://www.inspectandadapt.com/blog/beware-white-knight
[4] User Stories Applied, Cohn, M., 2004, Addison-Wesley
[5] Product Mastery: From Good to Great Product Ownership, Watts, G., 2017, Inspect & Adapt Ltd.

Tactful
[1] Agile Project Management with Scrum, Schwaber, K., Microsoft Press, 2009
[2] Collaboration Explained: Facilitation Skills for Collaborative Leaders, Tabaka, J., 2006, Addison-Wesley
[3] http://en.wikipedia.org/wiki/Parkinson's_law
[4] http://agilemanifesto.org/principles.html

Resourceful
[1] http://en.wikipedia.org/wiki/Bullshit_bingo
[2] http://www.agilify.co.uk/resources/
[3] The Art of Focused Conversation: 100 Ways to Access Group Wisdom in the Workplace, Stanfield, R. B., 2000, New Society Publishers
[4] http://www.youtube.com/watch?v=cXuD2zHVeB0
[5] Project Retrospectives: a Handbook for Team Reviews, Kerth, N., 2001, Dorset House
[6] Agile Retrospectives: Making Good Teams Great, Derby, E. & Larsen, D., 2006, Pragmatic Bookshelf
[7] http://en.wikipedia.org/wiki/Hook_(filmmaking)
[8] Innovation Games: Creating Breakthrough Products Through Collaborative Play, Hohmann, L., 2006, Addison-Wesley

Alternative
[1] https://www.ted.com/talks/tom_wujec_build_a_tower_build_a_team
[2] http://tastycupcakes.org/2013/05/the-penny-game/
[3] T-Shaped Stars: The Backbone of IDEO's Collaborative Culture, Hansen, M. chiefexecutive.net, http://bit.ly/139qdQX
[4] http://jeffsutherland.org/2003_03_01_oldstuff.html
[5] https://twitter.com/estherderby/status/304586137865945088
[6] Team Mastery: From Good to Great Agile Teamwork, Watts, G., 2020, Inspect & Adapt Ltd
[7] http://en.wikipedia.org/wiki/test-driven_development
[8] Slack: Getting Past Burnout, Busywork, and the Myth of Total Efficiency, Demarco, T., 2001, Dorset House Publishing

Inspiring
[1] https://www.youtube.com/watch?v=pvdCFYLf_JI
[2] https://www.youtube.com/watch?v=8xZm2UOam74
[3] http://growingagile.co.za/2012/03/make-work-fun/
[4] http://tastycupcakes.org/2012/11/delight/
[5] Drive: The Surprising Truth About What Motivates us, Pink, D., 2011, Canongate Books Ltd
[6] https://www.ted.com/talks/dan_pink_the_puzzle_of_motivation

Nurturing
[1] Coaching Agile teams, Adkins, L., 2010, Addison-Wesley
[2] Team Mastery: From Good to Great Agile Teamwork, Watts, G., 2020, Inspect & Adapt Ltd
[3] https://blog.odd-e.com/basvodde/2011/02/history-of-nokia-test.html
[4] Kahn, William A. (1990-12-01). "Psychological Conditions of Personal Engagement and Disengagement at Work". Academy of Management Journal. 33 (4): 692–724.

Empathic
[1] http://en.wikipedia.org/wiki/empathy
[2] The 7 Habits of Highly Effective People: Powerful Lessons in Personal Change, Covey, S., 2004, Simon & Shuster
[3] Coaching Agile Teams, Adkins, L., 2010, Addison-Wesley
[4] http://tastycupcakes.org/2012/03/one-word-storytelling/
[5] http://tastycupcakes.org/2012/11/three-headed-expert/
[6] http://tastycupcakes.org/2012/10/story-spines/
[7] http://tastycupcakes.org/2012/10/first-letter-last-letter/
[8] http://tastycupcakes.org/2012/03/one-word-storytelling/
[9] https://youtu.be/cbbl_XvTBEY
[10] https://www.estherderby.com/inflicting-help/
[11] https://www.performanceconsultants.com/grow-model
[12] https://youtu.be/-2lmBXvRZGk
[13] Team Mastery: From Good to Great Agile Teamwork, Watts, G., 2020, Inspect & Adapt Ltd

[14] https://en.wikipedia.org/wiki/Endowment_effect
[15] https://www.reference.com/business-finance/organizational-politics-df167f40b547fd36

Disruptive
[1] Succeeding With Agile: Software Development Using Scrum, Cohn, M., 2009, Addison-Wesley
[2] https://www.organic-agility.com/

Have BELIEF
[1] http://en.wikipedia.org/wiki/Pygmalion_effect

Notes

Made in the USA
Middletown, DE
15 November 2022